"A work of this caliber is long overdue. *The Warrior Method* is a must-read."

—Dr. Henry Foster, former senior advisor to
President Clinton on teen pregnancy reduction and youth issues

"An important book appearing at a crucial time . . . as we struggle to raise healthy black men in an unhealthy society."

—Jill Nelson, author of *Police Brutality: An Anthology*

"*The Warrior Method* is a sonnet, a love poem, to the lost sons of Africa."   —Harry Allen, founding member of Public Enemy

"[Winbush] provides guidance for anyone committed to helping young black men improve their knowledge and behavior in spite of insurmountable obstacles."

—Samuel Hingha Pieh, great-grandson of
Joseph Cinque, leader of the *Amistad* Rebellion

"If you care about the future of young black sons and brothers, *The Warrior Method* provides deliverance."

—Deborah Mathis,
nationally syndicated columnist, Gannett

"Clear, concise, and insightful. This book should truly be close at hand to anyone committed to raising black boys."

—Molly Secours, counselor to at-risk teens
and incarcerated youth

"Dr. Winbush has proven that it takes the men and the women in the village to raise strong black children."

—Yvonne Scruggs-Leftwich, PhD,
executive director/COO, Black Leadership Forum Inc.

The
Warrior
Method

The Warrior Method

UPDATED EDITION
A PARENTS' GUIDE
TO REARING HEALTHY
BLACK BOYS

Raymond A. Winbush, PhD

Amistad

An Imprint of HarperCollins*Publishers*

A hardcover edition of this book was published in 2001 by Amistad, an imprint of HarperCollins Publishers.

HarperCollins books may be purchased for educational, business, or sales promotional use. For information, please e-mail the Special Markets Department at SPsales@harpercollins.com.

FIRST AMISTAD PAPERBACK EDITION PUBLISHED 2002.

UPDATED EDITION PUBLISHED 2018.

Designed by Kate Nichols

Printed on acid-free paper

The Library of Congress has catalogued the previous edition as follows:

Winbush, Raymond A. (Raymond Arnold), 1948–
     The warrior method : a program for rearing healthy Black boys / Raymond A. Winbush.—1st ed.
          p. cm.
     Includes bibliographical references and index.
     ISBN 0-380-97507-6 (acid-free paper)
     1. African American boys—Social conditions.   2. African American teenage boys—Social conditions.   3. African American boys—Conduct of life.   4. African American teenage boys—Conduct of life.   5. Child rearing—United States—Handbooks, manuals, etc.   6. Child rearing—Africa, West.   7. Poro (Society).   I. Title.

E185.86.W556 2001
649'.15796073—dc21   2001022335

ISBN 978-0-06-283887-2 (pbk.)

18 19 20 21 22 DIX/LSC 10 9 8 7 6 5 4 3 2 1

To the Winbush men in my life who have made a
    difference:

Dad, who is with the Ancestors
Faraji, my youngest son who has taught me so much
    about being a father
Omari, my oldest son whose gentle spirit has been
    my teacher
Ron, my brother and best friend who has joined
    my Dad
Nick, my nephew who has unbounded energy in all
    that he does
Windy, my brother who is also with Dad

To all the Winbush men, both living and with the
    Ancestors, this book is for you and reflects the love
    you give me . . .

Contents

Preface

On a sunny, palm-covered road during the spring of 1839, Seng-beh Pieh, his wife, son, and two daughters set out from their farm in Sierra Leone for a neighboring village. Suddenly four black men rushed out of the forest and ambushed them. Seng-beh's wife was smashed across the face as she struggled, and the children cried out as they watched their father dragged away. Slavery was not unknown in this region, and Pieh, who would be renamed "Joseph Cinque" by his captors, had been warned about the dangers of enslavement by Europeans and the small group of brainwashed Africans collaborating with them in the hellish enterprise. Torn away from his wife and children, Seng-beh, the son of a Mende king, was beaten into submission and taken to Lomboko Island, an infamous slave port a few miles off the coast of Sierra Leone. There he was sold to a wealthy Spanish trader, then chained below the deck of the slave ship *Iesora* to begin the horrific Middle Passage to the Caribbean. Cooperation with whites during the European enslavement of

Africans is often discussed, but rarely understood. These discussions usually accuse Africans of being responsible for their own enslavement because of their minor participation in this crime against humanity. Slavery created an entirely new class of Africans who sold and traded human beings as readily as they sold and traded cocoa and groundnuts. Over the years, many whites have asked me with feigned curiosity, "Weren't the Africans themselves responsible for slavery, since they sold their own people to Europeans?" I am quite sure that when they ask this question, they are seeking partial absolution for the sins of their ancestors. When black people ask it, I shake my head and wonder if they are direct descendants of Mayagilalo, the African responsible for Cinque's capture on that fateful day. What is exaggerated about African complicity in the slave "trade" is that Africans did not have much choice in the matter. This is similar to making the indigenous people of the United States who scouted for Custer responsible for the establishment of reservations in Montana years later. These questioners would have us think that the entire population of the west coast of Africa, where most blacks in the *Maafa na Maangamizi** originate, was involved with the slave trade. The fact is that very few Africans were directly involved, and the tiny minority who were could not have done it without the absolute cooperation of Europeans. The converse is not true. Europeans had the power to get their workers with or without the cooperation of Africans. They needed laborers, and Africans were available. The deraci-

---

* A Kiswahili phrase translated as "disaster" (*Maafa*) "and" (*na*) "great disaster that is intentional and continues" (*Maangamizi*) increasingly used by the global African community to describe the horrors and impact of enslavement. The phrase denotes the *continued* suffering endured by Africans throughout the world, is not confined to one historical event, and will be used throughout this book.

nated West Africans collaborating in the slave trade found cooperation with the Europeans at first difficult, eventually easy, and
ultimately destructive.

What is most amazing about the Middle Passage is that anyone survived at all. Eyewitness accounts of the voyage are filled
with descriptions of death, disease, rape, and torture. Rebellions
by the enslaved Africans were frequent but mostly unsuccessful,
and the panic that gripped the captives was nearly matched by
the crews who lived in constant fear of insurrections. About
three hundred people from various parts of West Africa were
crowded aboard the *Iesora*. Voices of Yoruba, Ibo, Akan, Wolof,
Ewe, and other Mende could be heard as the angry and frightened Africans made their way through the "doors of no return."
These doors were chiseled into the dungeons where Africans
were held before being crammed aboard the slave ships that
distributed them in South America, the Caribbean, and North
America. The doors were usually about five feet high and two
feet across so that only one African could move through at a
time, making it easier for them to be counted. Blood can still be
seen on the stone walls of the dungeons. Scars crisscrossed the
doors where the Africans clawed at the wood and resisted their
captors as they were stuffed into dungeons reeking of filth and
populated by vermin in the Castles of Ghana and the infamous
enslavement port at Gorée Island off the coast of Senegal. This
was their last view of Africa as they began the Middle Passage.
Cinque grew up hearing tales about how the white man ate Africans, and many of the captured men and women believed that
these people were from a land where food was scarce. Cinque
must have thought of this, but wanted desperately to believe
his elders who told him that the lands beyond the seas needed
workers. He and his fellow captives must have wondered what

type of work the white man was doing that he needed to travel so many moons to steal black people away from their families.

The worst part of the two-month voyage was the stench aboard the ships. A consistent thread that runs through all of the narratives written by captors and captives is the ever-present "bloody flux," a severe form of diarrhea that afflicted both slaver and slave. The Africans ached for the cool rivers of their villages to wash away the odor and filth that blackened their skin even further. The heat at this time was often unbearable, only worsening the smell of the waste, blood, vomit, and flux. The human cargo must have thought that God had forsaken them. Head and pubic lice added to their torment. Though the sexes were separated, the men could hear the women's cries of pain and agony as the sailors and captains casually raped and sodomized them. Many of the men and women prayed to their ancestors asking them to join them; and as the ship tossed back and forth on the waters on rainy days, Cinque's thoughts must surely have turned to his wife and children, who by now had been separated from him for two weeks. About two hundred aboard the ship survived the journey.

Three months later Joseph Cinque was sold in Havana to Jose Ruiz and Pedro Montez, wealthy Spanish plantation owners who lived in Porto Principe, a Cuban town about three hundred miles from Havana. Cinque and his comrades were purchased in early June 1839, and at eight o'clock on the evening of June 28, he and fifty-two other Africans were marched aboard the chartered schooner *Amistad.* Captain Raymond Ferrer, a small crew of two sailors, a sixteen-year-old cabin boy named Antonio, and a "mulatto" cook named Celestino set sail for the two-to-three-day journey to Porto Principe. The Africans were left unchained in the hold of the ship; whether this was due to Ferrer's incompetence or ignorance, it watered the seeds of rebellion already growing among the captive Africans. Except for the uncomfortable iron collars around their necks, the Africans were free of shackles. Confidence in his small crew and the chained hatch that held the human cargo during most of the journey probably led him to believe that rebellion was only a remote possibility. I believe that Ferrer's arrogance led him to think that by the time the Africans had gotten used to their "freedom" below deck, they would be in Porto Principe. Cinque was increasingly restless for the desired rebellion that must have been rolling around in his head for nearly three months. Certainly, the conditions on the *Amistad* were far better than on the *Iesora,* but during the months of his ordeal, he learned to be skeptical about anything the white man offered him, even if it seemed better than the previous evil. He refused to adapt to conditions that were not of his making and in later testimony would tell how much he worried about his family during his ordeal. Freedom for Cinque would always be more than simply sleeping unshackled below the deck of a ship.

Ferrer, a seasoned captain, told Ruiz and Montez that the journey would take two days. Almost immediately upon leaving Havana, the sky began to darken and the wind was replaced by a sweltering haze. Captain Ferrer decided to steer the sleek black schooner along the Cuban coast to its destination. This sailing course, he thought, would allow him to pull into shore quicker than if he were out on the high seas; British warships were known to seize Spanish vessels on a whim looking for illegal contraband and evidence of enslaved Africans. On the second day of the journey, fearing that the supplies would run out, Ferrer ordered the slaves' provisions cut, reducing the Africans' already meager rations by half. Ferrer began to worry about the restlessness of his human cargo as the wind blew against the *Amistad*'s sails, further extending their journey. Anxious as he was to rid his ship of the enslaved, he was still reluctant to turn out to sea because of the British warships, so he kept the *Amistad* hugging the Cuban shore and opted for the slower journey with less wind.

On July 1, four days into his journey, Cinque's anxiety was further fueled by Celestino, who played a nasty trick on him. Cinque asked the cook what was going to happen to them when they reached their destination. In answer, Celestino pointed to a row of beef-filled barrels, placed the knife he'd been using to chop vegetables against his throat, and pretended to slice it. Cinque's blood ran cold. This gesture confirmed his fear that white men ate Africans due to a shortage of meat in their homelands. Thoroughly taken by Celestino's cruel charade, Cinque decided that he'd rather risk his life than take the chance that Celestino was right. Walking away from the cook, Cinque spied a loose nail in the deck of the ship and hid it, hoping that he could use it as a key to the shackle around his neck. Later, working with his close friend Grabeau in the darkness below the deck, they managed to free themselves and the others. They crept stealthily into the kitchen and made weapons of the sugarcane knives that would now never be used by them in the cane fields.

At 4:00 A.M. Ferrer was jolted awake by shouts and screams on the upper deck of the ship. Jumping from his bed, he ran out of his cabin, only to be stopped by Cinque brandishing a cane knife. Ruiz and Montez, also awakened by the commotion, ran from their cabins and saw Cinque advancing on the captain. According to Ruiz's later testimony, Ferrer produced a dagger from below his tunic and, foolishly thinking that Cinque wanted more food, yelled at the slave owner to throw him some bread.

Cinque looked contemptuously at the basket of bread, then
ignored Ferrer's dagger, swung the sugarcane knife, and struck
a ferocious blow to the captain's arm. Cinque then ordered his
comrades to strangle the captain while he lay writhing on the
floor. The entire battle was over in forty-five minutes. Gesturing
emphatically to the captured crew, Cinque made his demands
known—Ruiz and Montez were to take them back to Africa
immediately.

The two took advantage of the Africans' ignorance of navigation; during the day they steered ever so slowly due east, but at
night, they maneuvered the ship north by northwest. After two
months of deceptive navigation toward the East Coast of the
United States, Cinque's hijacked ship was forced into port off
the shores of Long Island. After eight weeks on the high seas,
the *Amistad*'s sails had been reduced to rags. Provisions were
low, and eight Africans had died after consuming medicinal supplies in an effort to quench their thirst. Coming ashore on Long
Island, Cinque and several companions agreed to surrender to
authorities, thinking they would be sympathetic to what had
happened to them during the past three months. These notions
were soon dashed when Lieutenant Richard Meade aboard the
U.S.S. *Washington* ordered the *Amistad* and its captives to be
taken to Connecticut, where slavery was still allowed.

The entire affair quickly escalated into an international incident involving the United States, England, Spain, and Africa.
Spain was outraged because their "property"—the *Amistad*
and its captives—had been illegally seized by Cinque. Sierra
Leoneans were enraged because one of their citizens had been
captured, even though the British had declared the capital
Freetown—and by default the entire country—a haven for run-
away Africans who had been enslaved. For the United States,

the *Amistad* Africans were not only stirring the national debate on slavery, but they were also fueling tensions with England, due to the imperialist tone of the 1823 Monroe Doctrine, and with Spain, because of the defeat of the Mexicans at the Alamo just three years earlier. A grand jury was quickly convened in Hartford, Connecticut, in late September 1839, before the dispute escalated irreversibly.

The ensuing two-year legal battles brought together some of the greatest legal minds of the day to decide the fate of the Africans who'd taken over the *Amistad*. Curious onlookers paid the equivalent of $1.90 in today's currency to view the Africans as they exercised in the yard of the New Haven prison where they were held. However, because of what they perceived as a daring and ingenious act, whites feared Cinque and held him in solitary confinement. Many comparisons were made between Cinque and Nat Turner, who only eight years previously had led on land a similar rebellion that claimed the lives of more than sixty whites. Grudging admiration from even the most hostile quarters was showered upon the "black pirate," who had almost immediately achieved mythical status throughout the United States.

There was no corridor of power untouched by the case, and Cinque and his companions were the catalysts for consolidating the fledgling abolitionist movement, which had been fractionalized by various ideologies ranging from the conservative writings of William Lloyd Garrison to the call for an outright slave rebellion by David Walker. This was America's first civil rights case, and the divided abolitionist movement united to free Cinque. They reasoned that if it could be proven that he was not "property," as the Spanish claimed, and was free to return to his homeland, the claim could then be made that all Africans in America should have the same free status. This rather naive view of the

American judicial system did not, of course, take into consideration the intractability of slavery and the racism that fueled it.

Lewis Tappan, one of the leaders of the burgeoning abolitionist movement and a wealthy businessman, hired the best lawyers to defend the captives and made sure that their case remained front-page news during the first trial. President Martin Van Buren, aiming to shore up his vote with the slaveholding states where legislators were unsure about his stand on slavery, failed in his attempt to transfer custody of the *Amistad* captives to the Spanish, since the United States had no formal extradition treaty with Spain. The Monroe Doctrine of 1823 had increased tensions between Spain and the United States considerably, since it stated explicitly that Spain was to curb its expansionism in the Caribbean and South America. It contained a message of solidarity between the North and South American continents that Spain resented, and attempts to resolve international law issues such as extradition were overshadowed by the anger felt by Spain toward America's alliance with Latin America. Spain was willing to go to war over the incident and, through its ambassador, Pedro Calderon de la Barca, issued four demands to Secretary of State John Forsyth regarding Cinque and the other captured Africans:

1st. That the vessel be immediately delivered up to her owner, together with every article found on board at the time of her capture by the *Washington*, without any payment being exacted on the score of salvage, nor any charges made, than those specified in the treaty of 1795, article 1st.

2d. That it be declared that no tribunal in the United States has the right to institute proceedings against, or to impose penalties upon, the subjects of Spain, for crimes committed on board a Spanish vessel, and in the waters of the Spanish territory.

3d. That the negroes [*sic*] be conveyed to Havana, or be placed at the disposal of the proper authorities in that part of Her Majesty's dominions, in order to their being tried by the Spanish laws which they have violated; and that, in the mean time, they be kept in safe custody, in order to prevent their evasion.

4th. That if, in consequence of the intervention of the authorities of Connecticut, there should be any delay in the desired delivery of the vessel and the slaves, the owners both of the latter and of the former be indemnified for the injury that any accrue to them.

> —Mr. Calderon to Mr. Forsyth, 6th September 1839, and translation. U.S. Congress. House. Africans Taken in the *Amistad*. 26th Congress, 1st session, 1840. H. Doc. 185.

Americans were split along sectional and racial lines over the decision. The New Orleans *Times-Picayune* referred to Cinque as a "black piratical murderer," while abolitionists considered him a hero. Several exchanges between Spain and the United States resulted in the United States having the last word by allowing the trial to proceed in Connecticut.

In November 1839, Americans throughout the United States read Cinque's testimony in rapt attention, and his words were well conveyed. His black translator, James Covey, was located by Professor Josiah Willard Gibbs of the Yale Divinity School, and spoke perfect English and Mende. A reporter for the *New Haven Daily Herald* wrote the following about Cinque as he gave his testimony:

This Cinquez [*sic*] is one of those spirits who appear but seldom. Possessing far more sagacity and courage than his race generally do, he had been accustomed to command. . . . His lips are thicker and more turned up than those of his race in general, but when opened display a set of teeth rivaling in beauty the most regular of those which we praise so much in Caucasian beauty. But his nostrils are the most remarkable feature he possesses. These he can contract or dilate at pleasure. His general deportment is free from levity and many white men might take a lesson in dignity and forbearance from the African Chieftain.

In January 1840, a miracle occurred: the Africans won. Judge Andrew Judson ruled in their favor and set them free. Cinque had echoed during the trial that "we are men, too!" and evidently Judson believed him when he noted that the Africans were born free and should remain such. It is clear from existing court records and newspapers that the reaction to the verdict was swift and divided on racial and sectional lines in a country wrestling with the problem of what to do with its enslaved Africans. Van Buren was incensed and, along with Spain, ordered an immediate appeal to the United States Supreme Court. Abolitionists Joshua Levitt and Lewis Tappan knew that they had to secure the services of an esteemed lawyer to argue the case; who better to do this than the venerable orator John Quincy Adams, former president of the United States. He took the appeal case reluctantly, now seventy-three years old and in ill health, and for the next year became thoroughly versed in the first civil rights case to reach the Supreme Court. His thirteen-hour-long presentation to the court in February 1841 was nothing short of brilliant, since it focused on the issue of property rights rather than the thorny issue of the legality of slavery.

> . . . [the Africans] were in distress, and were brought into our waters by their enemies, by those who sought, and who are still seeking, to reduce them from freedom to slavery, as a reward for having spared their lives in the fight. If the good offices of the government are to be rendered to the proprietors of shipping in distress, they are due to the Africans only, and the United States are now bound to restore the ship to the Africans and replace the Spaniards on board as prisoners.
>
> > —John Quincy Adams. Argument before the Supreme Court of the United States in the Case of the United States, Appellants, vs. Cinque and Other Africans Captured in the Schooner Amistad (Delivered 24 Feb. and 1 Mar. 1841). New York: W. W. Benedict, 1841.

One week later, on March 9, 1841, the justices upheld the verdict of the lower court. Several of the Africans thanked Adams for his help. Letters by two of the captives, one by Kali and one signed by Cinque, containing his only extant handwriting, are especially noteworthy:

Mr. John Q. Adams

Farmington, May, 5th, 1841

Dear Friend.
We thank you very much because you make us free because you love all Mende people. They give you money for Mende people and you say you will not take it because

you love Mende people. We love you very much and we
will pray for you when we rise upon the morning and when
we lie down at night. We hope the Lord will love you very
much and take you up to heaven when you die. We pray
for all the good people who make us free. Wicked people
want to make us slaves but the Great God who has made
all things raise up friends for Mende people. He give us
Mr. Adams that he may make us free and all Mende people free. Mr. Adams we write our names for you

Kali

Mr. Adams
We write our names for you in this Bible that you may
remember Mende people. Some cannot write so we write
for them.

(Signed)

Kali   Cinque   Cici   Kinna   Falanna
Burmah   Fagino   Batu

Though Cinque and his brothers and sisters were finally set
free, their ordeal was far from over. Van Buren, apoplectic in
the White House at the verdict, refused to grant the freed Africans passageway home. The American Missionary Association
(AMA), formed by Tappan and other abolitionists during the
trial, became responsible for raising money to secure passage
back to Sierra Leone. In its most famous work, the AMA was
to establish several historically black colleges and institutions
throughout the United States: most notably, Atlanta University, Fisk, Talladega, and Tougaloo. Cinque and several of the
other Africans raised money for the journey home by touring the

northeastern United States for nearly a year. The "lecture tour" took on a sideshow appearance in some cities, because curious onlookers simply wanted to see the Africans speaking English. In November 1841, after earning the money for the passage home, Cinque and several other Mende set sail for Sierra Leone. They arrived there in January 1842, two and a half years after being forced into slavery. He never saw his wife or daughters again, but late in life he reunited with his son, Kolima.

Joseph Cinque's spirit lives on in his sons, America's African American men and boys. Historians are divided as to whether or not he was aware of the events that took place in the United States after his return to Sierra Leone. We are sure that he knew about the founding of several universities because of the American Missionary Association's efforts to educate the newly freed slaves. Surely, he must have known about the end of the American Civil War that "emancipated" his brothers and sisters still chained to the land that held Africa's descendants. Perhaps he was also aware of the rise of the Ku Klux Klan, which was lynching his sons, brothers, daughters, and sisters and the Jim Crow laws that were disenfranchising them from all institutions. He would be surprised, however, to see how his children have fared since his death a little over a century ago. . . .

Prologue

I am pleased to introduce *The Warrior Method,* a very timely and pertinent book, a tool to help inspire and motivate our young American African men to engage themselves constructively in positive choices in spite of what may seem to be insurmountable obstacles. Nothing is permanent because change is inevitable; therefore, we must not only anticipate change but also facilitate it. This is something *The Warrior Method* can do —help facilitate change in America.

The plight of our young men globally is precarious, and we must make a concentrated effort to redirect the path to adulthood that many of our sons are taking. As elders, we must become positive role models for our youth if they are to be future leaders. We must facilitate programs and teach from our own experiences to enhance their knowledge, attitude, and action toward family in particular and toward society in general. This knowledge must be packaged into "education for service" that we can then use to improve the quality of life for our society and ourselves.

Our sons' education should be shaped by an attitude that enhances their self-esteem and their self-actualization. Lessons from history, like the story of Sengbeh Pieh, who was called Joseph Cinque in America, and his colleagues, should motivate them to analyze their situation more critically and take calculated risks to improve their chances of success. Improving and expanding our knowledge of our history, understanding our contributions to America and the world, and combating the many fallacies surrounding black men in America will not only enhance our attitude but will also ensure that we are less destructive to ourselves and our community.

Knowledge, attitude, and responsible action will not only enhance the quality of life for individuals, but also invariably enhance the quality of life for all people. Miseducation and brainwashing are strategies societies use to conquer and control people and then exploit their resources for economic gain. Slavery brings with it not only physical chains but psychological chains as well. These psychological chains then form a link from one generation to the next, enslaving minds while restricting freedom. With knowledge and perseverance, people will take risks, even with fate. We must now take advantage of opportunities that will empower us to take back what is rightfully ours, take full advantage of our gifts as a people and a race, and direct our young men not only to achieve the glory of their ancestors but to surpass it. The key to the shackle around your neck is within your reach. It always has been.

It is time to take charge of our lives and to redirect the course of our sons' lives. It is never too late. My great-grandfather

Sengbeh Pieh chose to change the direction of his life's journey even though the odds seemed insurmountable. With one decision, Rosa Parks changed not only the course of her life but also the course of history. If each one of us chose to change the course of just one young man's life, we would ultimately change the course of American history and our place within it.

Eliciting this change can be as simple as looking toward Africa. Many good things and people have come out of the Motherland. The Margai family led Sierra Leone to independence from the British. The Carew family led the Sierra Leone United Methodist Church Conference to independence from America. The Nkrumah family led the independence movement in Ghana and in most West African states. The Piehs are distinguished in many fields such as education, public administration, medicine, public health, customer relations, criminal justice, and religion. All of Sengbeh Pieh's descendants continue to influence lives, even in America today.

Sengbeh and his colleagues were agents of change in world history. By seizing the moment, Africans ignited the revival of the abolitionist movement, which was nearing collapse due to competing ideologies. The case of Sengbeh Pieh and his colleagues, commonly referred to as the *Amistad* case, is regarded as America's first civil rights case. This case facilitated unity among the divided abolitionist movement whose influence on education and freedom of Africans worldwide is still felt today. Educational, religious, and spiritual institutions evolved in West Africa and the southern states of America as a result of the *Amistad* case. It was because of this coalition and partnership with other people of conscience that Sengbeh and the other Africans were able to return home. It takes a village of people who want to improve quality of life for the entire community to raise productive children. The responsibility is great but not impossible because, as the *Amistad* case teaches us, anything is possible.

Though Sengbeh lost his wife and daughters, he was able to reunite with his son, Kolima. Later they would evangelize the Mende people. Sengbeh had a lot of difficulties trying to represent Europeans to his Mende countrymen. His frustration and disappointment forced him to retire into the Sherbro land in southern Sierra Leone where he is reported to have died in 1879. Kolima and his wife, Mee kema, were caught up in the Hut Tax war with the British in 1898. Several American missionaries were killed on the bank of the Taia River in Mende land. Only Peter, one of Kolima's children, attended mission schools in Taiama and Rotifunk. Peter went on to teach in the American Missionary Schools, where he served for over twenty years and later became a pastor himself. Today, Taiama has a primary school, secondary school, and the largest United Methodist church in Sierra Leone. From all indications, the efforts of the first American missionaries who returned to Sierra Leone with Sengbeh Pieh and the other Africans were the reason that the mission work in Sierra Leone became sustainable. Most of the early Europeans died, but the American African missionaries survived and helped Sengbeh and the others venture out into Mende land. If you believe in freedom, then you must promote it; you must not rest until all enslaved people, whether physically, spiritually, or mentally enslaved, enjoy all its privileges.

Samuel Hingha Pieh
Great-grandson of Sengbeh Pieh

Introduction

> *In these bloody days and frightful nights when an urban warrior can find no face more despicable than his own, no ammunition more deadly than self-hate and no target more deserving of his true aim than his brother, we must wonder how we came so late and lonely to this place.*
> —MAYA ANGELOU

A National Crisis?

The cultural and social obstacles facing young American African males today are huge and vastly different from those of the last century. If the current rate of homicidal violence among black males existed in white males, a national crisis would be declared, followed by a White House conference to address the problem. According to the Centers for Disease Control and Prevention, black males die at eight times that of white males because of homicidal violence. Furthermore, the criminal prosecution—or is it persecution?—of black males continues unabated.

In 2016, the Sentencing Project, which keeps track of incarceration rates by race and offense, reported that overall, black men are nearly six times as likely to be incarcerated as white men. Of black men in their thirties, one in every ten is in prison or jail on any given day.

RATE OF IMPRISONMENT PER 100,000, BY GENDER, RACE, AND ETHNICITY, 2015

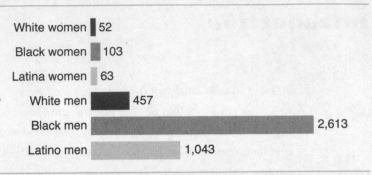

White women 52
Black women 103
Latina women 63
White men 457
Black men 2,613
Latino men 1,043

Source: Carson, E.A., and Anderson, E. (2016). *Prisoners in 2015*. Washington, DC: Bureau of Justice Statistics.

Marc Mauer in his 2011 article *Addressing Racial Disparities in Incarceration* found that African American males are more likely to be convicted and, once they are, more likely to face harsher sentencing. They are six times more likely to be imprisoned than white males and 2.5 times more likely to be jailed than Latinos. If current trends continue, one of every three black American males born today can expect to go to prison in his lifetime, as can one of every six Latino males—compared to one of every seventeen white males.

The likelihood of going to prison varies greatly by gender and race for those born in 2001. While critics of these data cite income and class as the primary reason for increased incarceration rates among men and women of color, Michelle Alexander in her book, *The New Jim Crow: Mass Incarceration in the Age of Colorblindness*, draws a straight and uninterrupted line between enslavement and the incarceration of American Africans. She argues that prison today is the equivalent of enslave-

LIFETIME LIKELIHOOD OF IMPRISONMENT FOR U.S. RESIDENTS BORN IN 2001

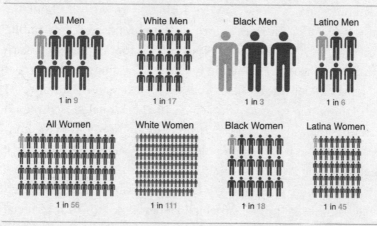

This estimate is based on data from 2001. Data source: Bureau of Justice Statistics.

ment and that laws locking up black men have a long history in American jurisprudence.

Few parents outside of the American African community truly grasp this reality, since violence is thought to be primarily a "black thing." When a black male commits a crime, it is expected; when a white male does so, it is explained.

Beginning with the 1999 Columbine school massacre, mass shootings were followed by this country's talking heads groping for a reason as to why young white males from the suburbs were killing their classmates. Dylann Roof, who slaughtered nine black parishioners in Charleston, South Carolina, during a Bible study in 2015, had a 12,000-word essay in *GQ* devoted to his upbringing and how he had "become a terrorist," including an in-depth analysis of the influence of his father on his beliefs. Contrast such analysis with that of Micah Xavier Johnson, a black man who killed five police officers in Dallas in 2016. He was referred to by the media as "callous," "animalistic," "heinous," and a "loner." Very little was discussed about his past except that he was an army veteran and had "few public posts on his Facebook page." No such elaborate analyses were offered by these same talking heads while explaining homicidal violence among young black men in Chicago and Baltimore. (I will later offer reasons why much of this violence is directed toward other black males.) Insofar as murder rates are concerned, there is a remarkable decrease since 1995 of black males victimizing one another.

In fact, there is more myth than reality surrounding so-called "black-on-black" crime, especially when it comes to interracial homicidal violence. Here are the facts according to the Uniform Crime Reports compiled by the FBI in 2013:

- Black-on-black homicides have decreased by 67 percent in twenty years, a sharper rate of decrease than white-on-white homicide.
- According to FBI statistics, 7,361 blacks were killed by fellow African Americans in 1991. In 2011, the number dropped dramatically to 2,447 African Americans.
- Among black youth, rates of robbery and serious property offenses are the lowest in more than forty years between 1970 and 2013.

The citation of these gloomy statistics is all too common when discussing black men, and I cite them here in order to redirect attention to how black males' self-destructive behavior can be attributed to the negative and stereotypical images bombarding them. Few people wish to make the connection between such self-destructive behavior and the images projected by the media and other sources, yet it is even more destructive for black men to ignore these connections.

Years ago, I was at an intersection near Fisk University and pulled up next to a young black man driving a late-model car. He gripped the steering wheel tightly, while simultaneously bouncing back and forth to the beat of the rap playing on his radio. I looked at him and smiled, and he returned the look with a scowl, yelling: "Mothafucka, what you lookin' at? I'll kill you!" He then gunned his car and took off. As I slowly drove off, I thought about what has happened to young brothers such as him, who think smiling is "soft," respect for elders is outdated, and eye contact means aggression. That thought was still with me when I got to my office. Instead of beginning my work, I sketched out some of the self-destructive and negative black male behavior I have seen.

Destructive Black Male Behavior

The Super Slaves

Black males who occupy high positions of authority yet are so infected by white supremacy that they work against freeing others from racial oppression. They are defined by whites as being "acceptable"; in the not-too-distant past they may have been seen as a "credit to their race." They define success as the degree to which they are disconnected rather than attached to American African culture, and find reinforcement for this in a nation that insists on blacks deracinating themselves in order to be "acceptable as Americans."

Hip–Hop Hustlers

Black males who rationalize violence and self-destructive behavior under the guise of "keeping it real." They see no connection between living the "thug life" and their obligations to black communities. In the mid-1980s, gangsta rap emerged as the background music for many hip-hop hustlers. It emphasized a lifestyle of materialism, denigration of women, and drugs. Fast-forward to the late 1990s and trap music took these destructive lifestyles to another level. Nihilistic behavior, including getting high on "lean," selling drugs, and objectifying women, led many to believe that hip-hop hustlers were encouraged by powerful entertainment executives to obliterate the political roots of hip-hop and weaponize hip-hop to further encourage self-destructive behavior among black youth. In this sense, hustlers of hip-hop include not only the performers, but also those behind the marketing of murderous and misogynistic music. I am an avid listener to hip-hop but am also critical of the negative influence some of its subgenres have had on black youth around the world. In working with young black males to analyze the lyrics and lifestyle of some hip-hop hustlers, I am always pleased at how astute young black boys are in deconstructing the negative influence of trap and gangsta rap. They readily see its seductive nature, especially when death and imprisonment accompany some of their favorite artists.

The Wanna–nevah–bees

Nearly deracinated, these persons have been variously referred to as the "black Anglo-Saxons" (Nathan Hare), "our kind of people" (Lawrence Otis Graham), and the "black bourgeoisie"

(E. Franklin Frazier). It is not an automatic state of mind when achieving the sacred middle class, but it can be the inevitable result of moving away from black communities psychologically, often physically, and resulting in cultural confusion about one's identity.

The Killers

The ultimate in self-destruction among black males, the males actually wreak direct destruction on black communities in the form of selling drugs, sex trafficking, or committing murder. They exhibit a near-total absence of protective behavior toward black communities and instead view them and their residents only in terms of exploitation.

What is important to note is that the self-destructive types listed above have always existed in the American African community. Even the Hip-Hop Hustler finds his ancestral linkages with the likes of minstrels who, though they have been romanticized as entertainers seeking to survive during the post-Reconstruction era, in many cases actively sought compensation and ignored the critics of the music they produced. Minstrels were merely black actors portraying the images that whites had assigned them, and many rap videos do the same with the images they show of young black men. There have also been black men who could easily be graduates of Poro Societies like Cinque, men who are representative of the best in black America and are not the exception.

Constructive Black Male Behavior

The Warriors

These black men directly engage white supremacist systems. They are the civil rights leaders, community organizers, writers, and artists who leave no doubt that their protest, writings, art, and action are antiracist. The Ethiopian word *Jegna* captures the meaning of this group of men. Psychologist Wade Nobles describes a *Jegna* as follows:

> A very brave person who is a protector of a culture, the rights of his or her people and their land.

> A *Jegna* is more than a "leader." She or he is someone who is not afraid to speak truth to power, is uncompromised, full of integrity and at the very core of his or her being sees the welfare and protection of their people as paramount. They are literally prepared to die for the community they represent. It refers to those who are altruistically committed, out of an unqualified duty to their people and nation, to teach our children the art and science of a politically conscious adulthood.

> —Wade W. Nobles, "From Na Ezaleli to the *Jegnoch*," in Lee Jones (ed.), *Making It on Broken Promises: African American Male Scholars Confront the Culture of Higher Education*, 2002.

Viewed by some whites and blacks as troublemakers, they see justice as a core value in their lives and speak out against various forms of racial injustice and protect their communities at all costs.

The Strategists

Viewed by some as "accommodationists," they are clear in their commitment to black people. They often hold positions of power and may be reluctant to take risks that involve the loss of power, but they will never work against their communities. They are the opposite of Super Slaves, who have no commitment to black people and, if given the opportunity, will actively work against their interests. Sam Greenlee in his important novel *The Spook Who Sat by the Door* tells how his character, Dan Freeman, infiltrates the CIA, learns its secrets, then organizes and wages war against racism/white supremacy with the knowledge he acquires.

The Healers

Educators, physicians, and ministers who equip black people with knowledge of self are healers. They focus on individuals rather than systems, but have a deep understanding of how systems work, particularly as they impact black people. They are black men and women who never miss an opportunity to provide encouraging words to victims of racism and give psychological direction to those confused by what is happening to them.

As an educator who specializes in the development of American African adolescents, I am constantly asked if there are any successful techniques to be used to help raise healthy, confident American African males. Of course. But it is far from easy, because psychologists and educators are reluctant to offer techniques that factor in the role of racism in the development of American African boys. The preferred method of explaining black male behavior is to focus on internal rather than external issues that determine their lifestyles. Social scientists who point the finger at white supremacy as a primary factor in shaping the development of black boys are perceived as being "too liberal" and avoiding the "hard questions" that focus on biological and intellectual inequalities in American African males. Furthermore, new research initiatives on understanding black boys continue to blame the victims. Several recent studies reflect the frustration of a society that feels this group of children has something so "wrong" with them that it offers biased research to "answer" some of the questions regarding them.

As recently as 2016, white scholars posit a genetic predisposition to crime and aggression, which they've dubbed the "warrior gene." Rose McDermott, a political scientist at Brown University, argues that "about 30 percent" of the general population possesses this gene (*monoamine oxidase A* or *MAOA*) that makes them especially prone to violence. It has been a topic of conversation on television talk shows such as *Dr. Phil* and also discussed in *National Geographic*, *Science*, and *Scientific American*. "Stressful environments" trigger this so-called "warrior gene," and therefore young black males who live in these communities may be genetically predisposed to crime.

Despite warnings from organizations such as the Genetic Literacy Project that try to educate the public on erroneous "scholarshit" (as my colleague Donna Ford of Vanderbilt University calls it), this research continues to flourish in laboratories around the world.

The politics of "black criminal behavior" even entered the 2016 national election when soon-to-be President Donald Trump erroneously (or deliberately) tweeted bogus "data" citing the nonexistent "Crime Statistics Bureau of San Francisco" that "81% of whites are killed by blacks." Though the "statistic" was totally false, Trump refused to retract it or apologize for reinforcing the stereotype of the "superpredator" black male cited by his opponent, Hillary Clinton, in a 1996 speech in New Hampshire. In a similar vein, Charles Murray and Richard Herrnstein's 1995 *The Bell Curve: Intelligence and Class Structure in American Life* offered a "social science" approach to intelligence and race that theorizes how social policy should be altered to allow for the intellectual "inferiority" of blacks and Latinos. It is clear that such biased research reflects a society seeking simple answers to very complex questions. It is also clear that American Africans are often used as scapegoats when public policy has failed to provide solutions to some of these problems.

Not so clear, however, is why explanations of white adolescent behavior are commonly offered in the context of how social forces shape their behavior. Mary Pipher's bestselling book *Reviving Ophelia* discusses how sexism plays a nefarious role in the development of white females, particularly as it relates to their dependence on male approval. It is nearly unthinkable to exclude social factors in explaining white adolescent behavior, yet explanations of black adolescent behavior often focus on the internal pathologies of black life in America. What is emerging is a picture of black adolescent boys that ignores how racism influences their lives. It is not black boys who must be examined, but child-rearing techniques that must be restructured so that these boys grow up healthy despite the racism that assaults them on a daily basis. What we have here is the classic question of what came first: the racist society or the dysfunctional black male?

The Poro and Sande Societies

Sengbeh Pieh and his childhood friends were fortunate to have been raised in the West African way of child rearing. The Mende created two secret societies that initiated their children into adulthood: Poro for boys and Sande for girls. When girls and boys reached their teens, they went through special training to join these organizations, learning everything that would move them into adulthood. Admission to both societies varied, with some emphasizing the ability to pay, and others opting for strong recommendations from older members' observation of certain children. Though these societies were not open to all Mende, if asked, children were encouraged to participate in this coveted rite of passage. Being a member of these societies guaranteed that the initiate would play an important role with the everyday governing of the Mende community. At age thirteen Mende boys wishing to become men paid a fee to join the Poro Society. The Sande Society taught Mende girls their responsibilities as wives, mothers, and members of the community. Older women taught the girls dancing and singing, domestic skills, child care, grooming, and etiquette, in addition to religious studies. The girls were initiated at menarche; as they grew older, they rose in rank within the society until they became a part of its administration. Adell Patton notes in his book *Physicians, Colonial Racism, and Diaspora in West Africa* that Sande-initiated women in Sierra Leone refused to allow African doctors to examine them unless they were Poro initiates.

During the Poro initiation, the boys were removed from their families for six months, from November to May, and taken by older men in the village to a remote area where they learned to

hunt, farm, cook, and protect their villages. The elders believed
that the boys should struggle to find answers about law, nature,
religion, and life itself, with adults guiding them only when necessary. Only in the past forty years have Western psychologists
proven that "active learning" is more instructive than passive
learning, which is directed by the instructor—something the
Mende learned a long time ago. The Poro Society taught not
only mental acuity but physical endurance as well. Its members
learned not only how to solve their own problems, but also how
to endure pain by sleeping at night with sticks that had been
soaked in water and placed under their bedclothes. They often
remained outdoors when it rained. Though harsh, their ritual
prepared the boys for survival under all circumstances. It con-
ditioned them to use whatever was at hand for food, tools, and
survival; and it taught them to see themselves as part of the environment rather than as a participant in it.

Poro Society also taught the young men to respect women,
since life flowed from the female. Poro teachings instilled a
sense of trust and mutual respect between African men and
women and ensured that women were free from male violence
and protected by all the men of their clan. The boys also learned
the importance of working closely with girls and women and
of the female's importance to the Mende culture. Both men
and women cooked the meals and helped to build the homes.
Though the boys' elders explained to them the roles of husband,
father, farmer, and hunter, the distinctions between male and
female roles in most West African societies were blurred and
in many cases nonexistent. In Poro and Sande Societies, the
initiates were taught all the laws of the Mende, such as their
responsibilities to their elders regardless of their medical condition. Poro also demanded that every law enacted by elders

in the Poro Society should be carefully considered and not just enacted because of self-interest or monetary gain. The societies also taught the laws and customs of other tribes and cultures, and the best way to navigate these laws in trade and other legal matters. To this end, mock trials were held in front of large audiences in order to increase the young boys' confidence in public speaking—something that served Sengbeh well when he became the central figure in America's first civil rights case. In sum, Poro Society taught young men to be *Jegnas*.

Poro Society is hundreds of years old and still exists throughout West Africa. In large parts of Guinea, Sierra Leone, and Liberia, all boys are expected to join the Poro of their local town or village when they turn thirteen. In *The Warrior Method*, I adapt parts of the Poro teachings as well as strategies specific for raising healthy black boys in our racist society. I make no apologies for arguing that white supremacy is the primary cause of problems encountered by them. There are other factors as well, but omitting it as a causal factor in their social growth is disingenuous and perpetuates the notion of black inferiority. Raising black boys in a racist society should be viewed as a challenge to the parent and educator who truly wishes to see healthy black men develop in the United States as well as in other Western nations.

A few years ago, after giving a lecture at the University of London, I was struck, but not surprised, as British educators and parents shared similar experiences about their black boys in terms of learning styles, violence, and rates of truancy. It is difficult for many people to accept that the treatment of black boys in predominantly white societies around the world is remarkably consistent. They experience high rates of expulsion from schools and police brutality, and they are viewed as being dangerous.

While it is easy to cite the pressures facing black boys, such as drugs, homicidal violence, and family breakdown, it is far less popular to discuss the roots of these challenges that emerge from other conditions sanctioned by racist societies.

My Own Story

Finally, the story of Cinque's sons is my story as well.

Evicted from four apartments in the years between 1950 and 1959, our family could have easily been the poster children for black poverty. In the late 1940s, my father was fired from his job at a Pittsburgh steel mill for organizing black steelworkers to resist taking the most dangerous jobs at the plants and advocating the revolutionary idea of "equal pay for equal work." In 1948, he moved our family to Cleveland to start a new life after being "whiteballed" throughout the steel industry in Pittsburgh. He joined that special group known as "bad nigger" men who were forced to leave small towns and cities quickly and often. Whenever they spoke truth to white power, they immediately lost their jobs and had to move on to find new employment, all at the whim of white supremacy.

Adding my youngest brother, Ron, to the Winbush brood broke him financially and resulted first in evictions and then in six heart attacks, the first in 1959. His anger and frustration at not being able to provide for his family were often taken out on our mother. My parents were constantly at odds over exactly what was causing their fighting and poverty. They simply didn't understand that their problems were inflamed by the racism around them. Low wages, a depressed economy, and discrimination were what contributed to the frustration between them.

They were able to see this when Malcolm X and Martin Luther King Jr. came on the scene and showed them—and the rest of black America—the enormous influence racism played in their lives.

Growing up on the east side of Cleveland during the 1960s, my brothers and I saw violence every day. We all coped with it in different ways. These different approaches created both harmony and friction between us as we tried to share elements of our vastly different worlds. I, the middle brother, had been fortunate enough to score high on what I later would know was the Stanford-Binet Intelligence Test. That score enabled me to be bused out of my poor neighborhood to an accelerated school in a middle-class white neighborhood. I often felt like the brother on the outside because of my privileged education at a well-kept, predominantly white school, far from the "horrors" of Hough Avenue. Ron, one year younger than me, was constantly fighting off neighborhood bullies throughout both junior high and high school. It troubled me that I went to school in a relatively safe neighborhood while he had to fight nearly every day just for the right to learn. He paid the price by making only fair grades during his middle school years, but he excelled academically in high school after our parents moved us to Warrensville Heights, a suburb that was safe, clean, and predominantly populated by working-class whites.

Academically, Ron was in a much better place, but now the violence came from his white classmates who resented the fact that their neighborhood was becoming a "promised land for blacks." Forced into a fight by the leader of a group of Italian boys who cornered him after school, Ron broke the jaw of one of the kids, which almost resulted in *his* suspension from school.

Although fighting almost every day, Ron somehow managed to finish high school with good grades. He went on to Cleveland State University, where he played varsity basketball. Maintaining his politics, Ron was arrested in 1970, as one of the "CSU Six," for demonstrating against neo-Nazis in support of the killings that took place at Jackson and Kent State Universities. He then graduated from college and went on to earn a master's degree in social work from Case Western Reserve University. He married a high school classmate and lived for the rest of his life in the upper middle class of fashionable Shaker Heights, Ohio. His untimely death from a heart attack in his late fifties shattered me. It followed my own heart attack while I was in my early fifties, and both illnesses reflected the stress that black men face in their everyday lives.

My brother Ron was living proof that one can be true to his politics and his people without sacrificing himself. The way Ron and I differed was that he threw the violence back into the face of whoever was dispensing it, while I tried to navigate around it by seeing it as symptomatic of what was happening to black people in general. I would later discover that both our strategies were invaluable for surviving as black boys growing up in America.

Our oldest brother, Harold, or "Windy" as we called him, was older than me by eleven years, and by turns both brilliant and contentious. Bored by the boring and laissez-faire Eurocentric curriculum and apathetic teachers in his Cleveland high school, he simply stopped going and instead turned to various forms of hustling and theft. His brief marriage at twenty-one resulted in divorce and a daughter. His many brushes with the law caused our parents endless grief. Some of my earliest memories of

Windy consist of our visits to see him at the Work House, a Dickensian slave camp where the crime of nonpayment of child support was punished by incarceration and fifteen cents an hour in wages until it was paid off. He left the Work House only to graduate to the state penitentiary, where he did five years for first-degree manslaughter. Windy had secured a job with the state branch of the mental hospital as an orderly. He viewed it as something that would enable him to rebuild his reputation, which had been increasingly marred by petty brushes with the law. As an orderly, he did mundane chores such as shaving, dressing, and taking care of mentally ill and disturbed patients who had varying grasps on reality. Though the work was menial, Windy was proud of having and keeping a job, and he always set out for work with a spring in his step.

One night, approximately three months into his job, one of Windy's patients started taunting him, calling him "nigger" and spewing racial epithets as Windy shaved him. My brother lost control, and the years of rage that he'd kept so tightly reined in slipped. I make no excuses for Windy. I simply know that he had seen violence firsthand, and when he reached his breaking point, he couldn't hold himself back. He let the ten years of frustration, disappointment, anger, yearning, and his feelings of lack of fulfillment take control of his reason. Windy did what many black men—who have simply been pushed too far—think about doing, but thankfully rarely do. For his crime, he spent five years in prison for first-degree manslaughter.

For weeks after Windy was arrested, there was an outcry against Ohio State mental facilities. The newspapers trumpeted the story of how the institution had entrusted the lives of patients to an "ex-con." Ron and I endured the taunts from

neighbors and classmates, and the drama created in me a distrust of "friends," who saw the manslaughter charges as a vehicle
to tease, mock, and humiliate me as the brother of a murderer.
I was involved in many fights during this time, and although I
never backed down, I knew I was caught up in a strange self-
fulfilling prophecy because I was reinforcing the misconception
that the Winbush brothers were simply violent black men.

I corresponded with Windy while I attended Oakwood
University. I always looked up to him—even when he was in
prison—because he was well read, had a sharp mind, and often
told me things that later came true. He warned me to be careful
with the white boys I would later meet at school because they
would try to make me feel inferior. He told me to read something every night about black people so that it would balance
the "poison" I would read every day about white people. He
also told me that debating taught one how others think: that I
should debate with people I didn't trust because it would teach
me more about them, and that I should avoid debating with
people I did trust because it might distance me from them.
He saw argument as a way of gaining knowledge and primarily
reserved for persons whom you either did not know or did not
trust. His knowledge and insight served me a world of good as
I made my way first through Oakwood, then Harvard and Yale
on summer scholarships, and finally through the University of
Chicago, where I got my master's and Ph.D. in psychology, and
where only eight blacks walked across the stage during my 1976
graduation ceremony.

In 1994, I had an eerie feeling of déjà vu while watching
the film *The Shawshank Redemption*. Staying for the credits, I
understood the feeling of recognition. The film had been shot

in Mansfield Reformatory, the now abandoned penitentiary in Ohio where I often visited my brother as he served his time. As the lights went up in the theater, I considered how ability and luck had played a major role in the lives of the Winbush brothers. Ron and I were lucky that civil rights legislation dismantled walls that had prevented Windy from even dreaming about college. He had gone to school just before Rosa Parks took her sheroic sit-down against racism on a Montgomery, Alabama, bus, and just before Ron and I got the largesse of a nation attempting to atone for the sins of its past. Our scholarships to Harvard, Yale, Cleveland State, Case Western Reserve, and the University of Chicago did not exist just ten years prior to when we attended school there, and Windy might not have gone to prison had he had the same educational opportunities afforded to Ron and me. What we had in formal education, Windy compensated for by being a voracious reader. He told me in a letter never to throw away a book because I could learn something from all of them, and that I may need that knowledge in the future. I retain this obsessive habit to this day. In a letter from prison to my sister Myrna, dated March 27, 1966, Windy wrote:

> One of the worst things that can happen to any individual is when a person's freedom is denied him, or taken away. I never realized the joy and pleasure of freedom until I came here . . . it's a hurting feeling to be stripped of my manhood and lose your identity as a human being . . . there are many in here who have peace with the world. Why? Because this is the only life they have known. These—vegetables, that's what they are to me—have no ambitions, no goals in life . . . I pity all of them. . . .

Even in the bowels of "Shawshank," Windy saw himself as better than other inmates, because prison for him was simply *where* he was and not *who* he was.

Black boys in the 1960s were members of the last generation of young men who had their eyes on the prize. As a group we knew where we were supposed to go, and how to get there. Like Windy, many of us may not have chosen the right path, or may have let circumstances get the better of us, but we knew that ours was the generation that was to fulfill the dreams of Du Bois, Crummell, and Garvey. They were our heroes. We mourned the death of JFK the way my father mourned the death of Roosevelt, but we did not name our sons "Kennedy" the way my father's generation had named their sons "Roosevelt," in tribute to their fallen hero. We changed our names to "Muhammad," "Kahlil," and "Amiri," and traded in our "slave names" for an "X."

Our eyes were turning east to Africa in ways that had not been seen since Marcus Garvey's Back to Africa movement in the 1920s. Black men were wearing dashikis, although no such clothes existed in Africa. We celebrated the naturalness of our kinky, nappy, and locked hair, and, finally, black became beautiful. West Africa was the place to vacation as much as Grandma's southern home during the summer. Cassius Clay became Muhammad Ali, and Stokely Carmichael took the name Kwame Ture, moved to Guinea-Bissau, and reinforced the idea that living in Africa was a viable alternative to living with the racism in America. In 1961, Du Bois moved to Ghana, and Nkrumah encouraged others to do the same. Black boys heard their fathers openly revere and criticize Dr. King, for they were both awed and appalled by his militant nonviolence.

The story of *The Warrior Method* is the story of all black

men in America, and their sons as well. My story, the story of three black boys growing up in Cleveland, Ohio, during the 1950s and 1960s, is one of opportunity, chance, and blind fate; it mirrors the experiences of all black boys in America. Though far more intelligent than I, Windy ended up in prison while I ended up at Harvard. Our fates were nothing more nor less than circumstances and opportunities. The opportunities given to Ron and me were a gift and a godsend, and they enabled us to live up to our potential. But we were two out of hundreds. I wonder what Windy would have done with them, who he would have become, what would have been his contributions? Opportunities like these—education, safe schools, a congenial learning environment—are the norm for white boys who are given the chance to succeed daily, while black boys have to fight daily, just for the right to learn or the chance to dream.

I wonder what America would be like today if all of Cinque's sons were given the opportunity and the resources for achievement? And I wonder what America will be like for my sons, Omari and Faraji. . . .

1

The Image of Black Males in American Society

Being a black man in America is like being a specta-tor at your own lynching. —ISHMAEL REED

Prisons Without Walls

I had just finished a daylong speaking engagement at a prison in a very rural area of south-central Tennessee. It was almost dusk as I made my final comments to a group of incarcerated black men. I listened to their stories about how they'd found themselves in this lonely rural place where the "strange fruit" of their ancestors had hung on trees in the not-too-distant past. As I said my good-byes, I was pleased that we'd all come to realize how much we had in common as black men. In addition, I was thrilled that they had entrusted me with information, greetings, and letters to send to their families, parole boards, and friends in the "free world." I, in turn, took their addresses and promised to keep in touch. I then said my farewells and started on my journey home, up the very dark and meandering road away from the prison.

It was in the "pre-GPS" era and I got lost almost immediately. The inky blackness of the Tennessee woods, complete with kudzu-laden trees, gave eerie shapes to the thick undergrowth hovering over the two-lane highway in the middle of nowhere. I made a decision to stop at the first light I encountered, which came after driving nearly five miles. I pulled into a country gas station and noted how fast the bugs were flying around the lights illuminating the convenience store. As I got out of my car, I suddenly felt more connected to my brothers whom I had just left. Inside the store I saw a white man with a red baseball hat, peering curiously through the window at me. I looked beyond him farther into the store and saw two white women sitting behind a counter. In that split second, it occurred to me that one of them was clutching an object beneath the well-worn table. I realized that the object was a gun and that I was dangerous in their eyes simply because I was a black man entering their store at night. To them I was out of context. It happens to black men when we drive into an all-white neighborhood, walk into a restaurant in an area where serving black men is both rare and unexpected, or simply when we try to get directions when lost.

I quickly "assumed the position," placing my hands where they could easily be seen on the glass door, and walked in. As I entered the store and casually asked the man for directions, I could feel the tension. His Tennessee drawl sketched a vague picture of where the interstate might be. While I listened, I suddenly realized that the only reason I had entered the store, after seeing their looks of fear, was to dispel the notion that I was intent on either robbing or killing them.

I thanked him for the directions, and then, without thinking, turned and asked the woman what she was holding behind the counter. I was surprised at my own words even as they left my mouth, knowing that my question could easily be interpreted as a way of sizing them up before I committed my crime. "A gun," she replied quite calmly. Stepping deeper into the racial abyss, I asked her if she thought I was going to rob her. In the same Tennessee monotone she answered, "Yes."

Her two companions moved closer to her behind the counter, and I recklessly continued. More from a race-fatigued haze than from bravado, I asked if she'd assumed, because I was black, that I was going to rob her. She paused a moment and, in a low voice, said, "To be honest, yes." They all looked at me, and for a split second, I could see plainly their embarrassment, anger, and bewilderment. I felt strangely empowered. Just a few moments earlier, I'd felt powerless and somehow at fault simply for being a black man. But as we all stood there looking at one another and barely breathing, I felt in control. I had reacted honestly when confronted by their discrimination and stereotypical images of black men. I took a breath and then asked if they could spare a few minutes to talk to me about what just happened, and what could have happened but thankfully hadn't. Surprisingly, they said they could.

Though I do not remember exactly the words exchanged during the next twenty minutes or so, what I do remember quite clearly is that all three talked extensively about how their impressions of black males had been formed by a witches' brew of stereotypes, television, folklore, hatred, and misunderstandings. They all had the same fears—due mostly to ignorance— of black-on-white crime and interracial sexual couplings. After we'd talked for a few minutes, they began to ask me questions that no one in their white world could answer with any degree of certainty or authenticity. They were curious to know my feelings about O. J., Tupac, Colin, Louis, Michael, and many other black males. As we talked, they expressed deep-seated beliefs passed on from their parents and peers, fallacies such as the black man's sexual and athletic prowess, his wanton and overriding lust for white women, and the black woman's sexual promiscuity. Neighborhoods will deteriorate and schools will decline if blacks were allowed to "move in," they told me. It seemed as if all of the misinformation they had heard and repeated to one another was now ready to be shared with the one black man who happened to wander into their store that night.

I listened closely to all that they said, and I realized that only a moment before these same people had been prepared to shoot me, and probably would not have gone to jail if they had. Their ignorance had made them just as afraid of black people in general, and black men in particular, as their predecessors had been when D. W. Griffith shot *The Birth of a Nation*, when the Scottsboro Boys were tried, when Emmett Till was lynched, or when Willie Horton became the poster child for black men. These people were afraid of me for no reason at all. And had it not been for my pausing to discuss their fears, they simply would have wondered what a black man was doing in "their" town so late at night, out of the context in which they had cast him.

After about twenty or thirty minutes, the man said, apologetically, that it was time to close the store. I embraced the idea quicker than the woman did, and said that I needed to be on my way before it got any darker. We lied to one another about stopping by if either was in the other's area. Then I walked into the cool night, glad that one more time I had escaped death from the hands of the white people who had stereotyped notions of black men. I know many black men who have had similar escapes, and I know of too many others who didn't.

If this incident had happened during the Trump era, the ending might have been far worse and the conversation much different. Perhaps the clerks would have shot me, and for sure, their conversation would have been far more aggressive and less inquisitive about Tupac and why "illegal immigrants" were taking away their jobs. Surely we would have discussed the police killings of Michael Brown and Philando Castile and how they might have been complicit in their own deaths.

The American propaganda machine has been thorough, on so many levels, in poisoning the minds of insecure whites about black males. The results of this stereotyping have yielded a complex web of images for black boys. In a 2014 study by the American Psychological Association, black boys were viewed as being older and less innocent than white boys. Much of this perceived "dangerousness" on the part of whites can be understood by anatomizing the nexus between race and sex in American history.

The Black Male as Sexual Predator

"Lazy," "shiftless," "violent," "gangsta," "hoodlum," "stud," "invisible," "stupid," "entertaining," "superathlete," "dangerous," "hypermasculine." If this were the extent of the list of adjectives and nouns used to describe contemporary American African males, perhaps young blacks could resist the powerful message it sends to them. Unfortunately, the list goes on and on. Black males grow up with the knowledge that society in general believes them to be mostly worthless if they are not superathletes or entertainers, and that they are limited in what they can achieve.

Every day nearly all forms of media assault American African boys with the notion that they are simply no good. Black men handcuffed on the eleven o'clock news, "gangsta" rappers with platinum fangs in their mouths, and exaggerated images of young black males being arrested for drugs provide daily doses of negative images to young black boys. Images that serve to reinforce negative stereotypes that black males are insane take the form of a racially/sexually confused Tyler, the Creator, a selectively amnesic Kanye West, and an army of rap artists who stare into the camera during their videos with threatening postures while they call black women "bitches" and "hos" and their brothers "dawgs" and "niggahs." The "thinking black male" is seen at best as quirky or at worst as an aberration. This "Urkelization" of intelligent black men is seen in Ving Rhames's portrayal of an electronic genius in the film *Mission: Impossible*. His character seldom speaks, is sexless, and has encyclopedic knowledge of the most esoteric of things. Although viewed as a "strong black man," he was gang-raped and sodomized by white men in the 1990s cult classic *Pulp Fiction*. Hollyweird, as Chuck D of Public Enemy calls it, has a way of whittling down even the strongest images of black men to blubbering and sexless creatures.

The elevation of George Washington Carver to mythic status by white teachers, while emphasizing pride in the genius of the "Wizard of Tuskegee," inadvertently portrays him as an *exceptional* genius with scientific feats that could hardly be duplicated by the average black man. Intellectual achievements of black men are not ignored; they are *exceptionalized* into the realm of the extraordinary. Even a young Tiger Woods, who fantasized about his "Cablinasian" ancestry in a sport that paid homage to intelligence, is not immune from sports commentators noting his "tremendous strength" in driving the ball, as opposed to the traditional references of "keen intellect" that are reserved for white golfers. Yet he, too, became the "typical black man," lusting after white women, and fell from white grace after his 2009 domestic quarrel with his white wife. Black NFL players are supposed to not *think* about the killing of black men and women by police but instead use their physical endowments to please crowds hungry to see black male bodies engaged in gladiatorial violence toward each other. If they become political by kneeling in their support for Colin Kaepernick, they can be called "sons of bitches" by the president of the United States. Wynton Marsalis's facility with both jazz and European classical music is seen as a "gift," even though Marsalis argues that a riff in jazz is far more difficult to play than a Bach fugue.

This disparagement of the black male intellect and the emphasis on his physical attributes have a long history. Their physicality is believed to be the only part of black men worth discussing. This constant and universal narrative began with the initial encounters that European explorers had with Africa. Winthrop Jordan, in his classic work *White over Black*, presents numerous documents written during the European colonization of Africa where explorers wrote back to their home countries about the extraordinarily "long tailes" of "wild" black men in the "jungles of black Africa."

Dr. Frances Welsing argues, as does Dutch scholar Jan Nederveen Pieterse in his book *White on Black*, that the sexual image of black men was unconsciously *and* consciously shaped by white men in literature, anthropology, and history to distort and particularly to exaggerate their prowess in order to create in white females the fear of rape by black men. He argues that "protecting white women"—a persistent theme in the history of European racism—is a reflection of the insecurity that white males have of the black penis.

This "black man will rape you" anxiety, a persistent American theme, was placed squarely at the forefront of American politics as far back as the 1988 presidential elections. The late Lee Atwater, campaign manager for George H. W. Bush, used it in the infamous Willie Horton political ads to swing the white "female vote," which had been leaning heavily toward Michael Dukakis. Horton, convicted of raping and killing a white woman during a weekend pass from prison, was employed in political ads that effectively siphoned white female votes away from Dukakis. In an interview with *Life* magazine just before his death, Atwater admitted that the ploy in the commercials was to present Dukakis as "being soft" on black criminals. Going for the racial jugular vein by presenting Mr. Horton as the embodiment of the Great White Fear—black men raping and killing white women—worked, swinging a significant portion of the female vote to George Bush. The rest is history.

Susan Gubar says that white parodies of black life are so endemic to America that they are unconsciously reflected in art, literature, and film. She cites the example of a colleague teaching at an Ivy League university who confided in her that her husband spoke "black talk" to their dog. She says that sexuality in particular creates anxiety among white Americans so much so that its expression is often difficult to discern. The denial of "black envy," as she calls it, borders on the pathological. She analyzes Robert Mapplethorpe's controversial 1980 photo *Man in Polyester Suit*, in which a black man clothed in a drab gray suit has his large penis hanging noticeably from his pants. Gubar argues that the black male is viewed with sexual envy throughout Western literature and that deconstructing this envy is often difficult since it challenges dearly held assumptions about black/white relationships both sexual and nonsexual. The O. J. Simpson murder trial provided yet another case of the unconscious obsession that white America has with the sexual dynamics of black men and white women. The so-called "race card" may be better identified as the "race/sex card" since these two powerful factors converged during this particular example of America's obsession with race and sex. The trial reinforced the notion that black male/white female sexuality is taboo because it is ultimately dangerous and often leads to death. In fact, only 3 to 4 percent of all rape is interracial (white men raping black women and black men raping white women) yet these are the cases that garner the most headlines. More than twenty years after the trial, white America remains fascinated with the race/sex dynamic of the O. J. Simpson trial as Golden Globes and Emmys were showered upon a 2017 miniseries depicting the trial.

Historically, the mere rumor of an interracial rape involving a black male and a white female could set the stage for a lynching. The fear of black men and white women coupling is a great determiner of social mores and shaped the image of black males in America. In 2014, Shannon Kepler, a white Oklahoma police officer, fatally shot a nineteen-year-old black man because he was dating his daughter. Convicted in 2017 of shooting Jeremey Lake, Kepler said that he thought Lake was threatening him with a gun. In reality, Kepler was enraged that his daughter Lisa was dating Lake, kicked her out of his home, and shot Lake after seeing him and his daughter walking near their home.

Bob Jones University's policy against interracial dating wasn't dropped until 2000 and was another indicator of white anxiety over black male/white female coupling. Despite the loss of federal funds in 1983 because of this policy, administrators at the university continued the long history of racism based on twisted interpretations of the Bible relative to "race mixing."

We should not, however, think that the "black male as rapist of white woman" fear is reserved only for white supremacists. Hollywood has consistently reinforced the notion of the black male as predator. D. W. Griffith's 1915 classic *The Birth of a Nation* was initially entitled *The Clansman*; the title was changed in part because he felt its appeal to Americans was far greater than the small sector of citizens found below the Mason-Dixon line. The appeal, of course, was to the primal fear in the American white psyche that black men will rape "our" fair daughters, wives, aunts, grandmothers, and sisters if they are not held in check. Woodrow Wilson, the Ku Klux Klan's favorite president, wrote in his *History of the American People* that the film showed "the policy of congressional leaders was determined to overthrow civilization in the South, to put the white South under the heel of the black South. For self-preservation, the whites formed a group called the Ku Klux Klan, a veritable empire of the South, to protect the Southern country."

The original *King Kong*, released in 1933, illustrates the symbolic anxiety over black male and white female sexuality. Released during the height of the "Scottsboro Boys" case, in which nine black boys and men ranging in ages from thirteen to twenty-one were accused of raping two white women, the film portrays a giant crazed ape lusting after a fair white woman in distress. Kong, who had resided peacefully in the African rain forest for an unknown period, suddenly goes wild (ape?) over a white female accompanying an expedition to his prehistoric island. Several authors have pointed out the nature of the phallus represented by the ape's ascension to the top of the then newly erected Empire State Building, and the subsequent killing of the monster by pilots is a symbolic castration and lynching of black men, still prevalent in America at the time of the film.

Far-fetched though it may seem, it provides an intriguing analysis of Hollywood's endorsement of the idea of black men as sexual predators. Lending credibility to this assertion is the fact that it was released in Nazi Germany during this same period as *King Kong und die Weisse Frau* (*King Kong and the White Woman*).

Although they exist, persons creating media images usually deny sexual/racial symbolism, even when symbolic references are far too blatant to overlook or ignore. The Planet of the Apes series, still going strong after fifty years, is a good example of black people as apes in a world where whites have lost control. The most overt depiction of black people as apes came during the Obama administration when literally hundreds of memes, cartoons, and editorials portrayed America's "first black president" and his family as apes. These symbolic and overt depictions of African people globally as animals continue the five-hundred-year-long denigration of black people as subhuman and worthy of ridicule and even extinction. The golliwog of the British, the Alabama Coon Jigger of America, and Black Peter in the Netherlands all represent the universal corruption of the black image by a system that demands white domination in all areas of social interaction including and especially the entertainment industry.

In his book, *Brainwashed: Challenging the Myth of Black Inferiority*, black advertising executive Tom Burrell says: "one of the greatest propaganda campaigns of all time was the masterful marketing of the myth of black inferiority to justify slavery within a democracy." I agree, and the result of this five-hundred-year advertising campaign was effective on the minds of all those exposed to the global system of white supremacy. It worked.

The portrayal of the black male as sexual predator has served well in convincing a sexually insecure white America that, if left unchecked, black boys will "marry our daughters." The horror! This unspoken social policy of racial exclusion based on gender and race placed black males in such a precarious position that we had to monitor even our most straightforward and innocent interactions with white women. The single most commonly given "reason" for the mass lynching of black men in America was the *idea* that they had violated white women by sexual molestation. Rumors alone were enough to ignite angry white men to *defend* white womanhood by lynching, burning, and castrating *any* black male perceived as having violated this code. The burning of the black section of Tulsa, Oklahoma, in 1921 and of Rosewood, Florida, in 1923, and the lynching of Emmett Till in 1955 are three of the hundreds of racial violence incidents that had their roots in the perception of black men as "violating the sanctity" of white womanhood.

The unconscious social fear of black men's libidinous urges toward white women is a globally held perception. From Shakespeare's *Othello* to the European exploitation of Africa, this theme is played out and is important in how racial policies are established. In hearings at the Truth and Reconciliation Commission, established by Archbishop Emeritus Desmond Tutu during Nelson Mandela's presidency, it was revealed that the primary obsession of the apartheid government of South Africa was to keep black men and white women away from one another. Similar to the situation in the United States, rumors of white women being harassed by black men in South Africa were met with swift retaliation by the government in the form of mass arrests and beatings.

This speech, given by South African president P. W. Botha on August 18, 1985, is quite telling:

. . . Our Combat Unit is now training special white girls in the use of slow poisoning drugs. Ours is not a war where we can use the atomic bomb to destroy the Blacks, so we must use our intelligence to effect this. The person-to-person encounter can be very effective. As the records show that the black man is dying to go to bed with the white woman, here is our unique opportunity. . . . We have received a new supply of prostitutes from Europe and America. . . .*

Embracing the Image

Reverend Eugene Rivers's *Boston Review* article entitled "Beyond the Nationalism of Fools" noted that black scholars such as Cornel West, Henry Louis Gates, and others, while discussing Marx, Hegel, Foucault, and Derrida, must devote attention to the plight of black boys only a few miles from Harvard but representative of young black males around the country. He cites the following data from the Children's Defense Fund:

A black boy has a 1 in 3,700 chance of getting a Ph.D. in mathematics, engineering or the physical sciences.
A black boy has a 1 in 94 chance of becoming a teacher.
A black boy has a 1 in 372 chance of becoming a lawyer.
A black boy has a 1 in 684 chance of becoming a physician.

* Rumors persist among South African blacks that paid white prostitutes (some with AIDS) were widely used by the apartheid regime. They were literally advertised for after they had contracted AIDS in places such as Amsterdam, New York, and London, and imported to South Africa.

A black boy has a 1 in 2 chance of not attending college,
    even if he has finished high school.
A black male has a 1 in 9 chance of using cocaine.

These statistics are a sampling of data on the state of young black
males in America. It has been an important task for American
policy makers to ensure that these data localize the "problems of
black males" squarely on the shoulders of black men, rather than
connecting the dots back to enslavement, failed social policies,
and systemic racism. Social scientists are often reluctant to discuss how rooted is the fear of black males in America and how
this fear is related to white sexual insecurity. It is a taboo subject,
with only a few persons daring to discuss it. Emerging as a recur-
rent theme in literature is the racist image of black people in the
white psyche, particularly in the area of blacks' sensuality and
their seeming "inability" to place intellect above bodily urges.
    Consider the source of the following quotations:

Among the blacks is misery enough, God knows, but no
poetry. Love is the peculiar oestrum of the poet. Their
love is ardent, but it kindles the senses only, not the imagination.

I think [a black] . . . could scarcely be found capable of
tracing and comprehending the investigations of Euclid.

. . . in this country the slaves multiply as fast as the free
inhabitants.

Their situation and manners place the commerce between
the two sexes almost without restraint . . . 567,614 inhab-

itants of every age, sex, and condition. But 296,852, the number of free inhabitants, are to 270,762, the number of slaves, nearly as 11 to 10. Under the mild treatment our slaves experience, and their wholesome, though coarse, food, this blot in our country increases as fast, or faster, than the whites.

—Thomas Jefferson, *Notes on the State of Virginia*, 1787

... the physical differences [which] will forever forbid the two races living together on terms of social and political equality. And inasmuch as they cannot so live while they do remain together there must be the position of superior and inferior, and I as much as any man am in favor of having the superior position assigned to the white race.

—Abraham Lincoln, 1864

The Negro is primarily affectionate, immensely emotional, then sensual and under stimulation passionate ... there is undeveloped artistic power and taste— Negroes make good artisans, handscraftsmen—and there is instability of character incident to lack of self-control, especially in connection with the sexual relation. ...

—Dr. Robert Bennett Bean, "Some Racial Peculiarities of the Negro Brain," *American Journal of Anatomy*, 1906

[T]he mental constitution of the negro is ... normally good-natured and cheerful, but subject to sudden fits of emotion and passion during which he is capable of performing acts of singular atrocity, impressionable, vain, but often exhibiting in the capacity of servant a dog-like fidelity which has stood the supreme test. . . . After puberty sexual matters take the first place in the negro's life and thoughts.

—Entry under "Negro," *Encyclopaedia Britannica*, Volume 19, 1911

These quotations are representative of the literature—both "scientific" and otherwise—that sought to instill a sense of inferiority in black people, and a sense of black people's "inferiority" in whites. Indeed, the persistent theme of Western civilization toward persons of color, blacks specifically, and black men in particular, is that they are sensuous and unintelligent creatures filled with unbridled lust. These assertions translated into public policies encouraging the emigration of black Americans to Africa; laws enforcing the separation of races, particularly of black men and white women; and broad, tacit endorsement of violence toward American Africans, particularly toward black men.

John Hope Franklin, in a stinging essay written for the nation's bicentennial, argued that the "moral legacy of the Founding Fathers" was the embedded racism stated explicitly in the Constitution and implicitly in the lives they led as slaveholders. The ripple effect of this legacy led to the Civil War, lynching, and enforced segregation that has been with us since the founding of the nation. What is more damaging, however, is how these racist views became the norm for how whites sexualized black men; their subsequent fears then determined how black males could be brutalized. Out of these attitudes would evolve an idealized black male that was overtly desexualized and would take the form of the watermelon-eating, slow-talking, and docile lackeys such as those portrayed by Willie Best and Stepin Fetchit during the 1930s and 1940s. His opposite would be the "bad nigger," epitomized by the blackfaced whites in *The Birth of a Nation,* and more recently by some rap artists in music videos.

The Consequences of Adaptation

To deny that the barrage of negative stereotyping has affected black male self-image is to ignore history and contemporary reality. Beginning with slavery, the need to survive forced many black men to adapt to white supremacist notions about themselves. This adaptation took many forms, such as engaging in little or no eye contact with more powerful white males and providing ego-boosting compliments to whites when they accomplished a minor feat. It is important to note that *not* recognizing the social cues provided by a white supremacist society in determining the status of black males could lead to premature death. My companions in the convenience store are the descendants of those who saw all black men as threats. Black men such as Emmett Till—more boy than man, actually—who did not recognize these cues were taught fatal lessons and used as examples for others who would transcend the unpredictable social barriers that were ever prevalent in Western society.

Imbibing the various identities assigned to them can be seen in the agony of Bert Williams as he performed in blackface during the early years of the twentieth century. It was seen in Mantan Moreland during the heyday of racism in Hollywood, and continued through the 1930s and 1940s with the tolerance of segregated entertainment in the Cotton Club and the "noble savage" characters portrayed by Sidney Poitier and Harry Belafonte in their earlier films.

After *Brown v. Board of Education* outlawed segregation in public schools in the United States, the images mutated into forms that were even more bizarre. Self-hatred became even more fashionable than it already had been among black men as evidenced in how we "did" our hair. It took on complex rituals after Madam Walker's invention of the straightening comb.

Malcolm X would analyze this in his autobiography as he "conked" his hair with lye to make it appear straight and more "white." It would continue with images of a bleached Michael Jackson and a blond Dennis Rodman, and reach its zenith with the racially unconscious lyrics of rappers such as 2 Live Crew and Too Short. What would be even more devastating is how the growing self-hatred among us would take the form of unprecedented violence between 1980 and 1995. Homicidal black-on-black violence reached an all-time high in 1993, with nearly two hundred black males (age eighteen to twenty-four) per one hundred thousand becoming victims, compared to only eighteen per one hundred thousand for white males during the same year. The recent dip in the homicide rate among young black males has been partially attributed to the "halo effect" of the October 1995 Million Man March. Those who are less inclined to give Louis Farrakhan credit for the declining rate attribute it to the roaring economy that characterized the last half of the 1990s, although this belies the fact that homicide rates rose steadily and consistently beginning in 1984 and ignored economic upswings. Perhaps the *greatest* indicator of self-hatred among black men is the two-thirds increase of suicide among black males age fifteen to twenty-four during the past fifteen years. Until 1980, black male suicide rates were some of the lowest in the nation, with suicide prevention programs viewing American African men as extremely "low risk." The increase in suicide among black males is exacerbated by the notion of what I call "homisuicidal behavior"—self-destructive behavior in which one consciously takes unnecessary risks. It is found in the young black man who knowingly flirts with danger by driving into inner-city neighborhoods occupied by rival gangs and flashing gang signs, or in the young black men who drive at high rates of speed without wearing seat belts. The rate of death in this group of black males, age thirteen to nineteen, is nearly twice as high as for a comparable group of white males. Black people are half as likely to be buckled in as whites or Latinos, according to a national study in 1999 by Meharry Medical College and General Motors. "Death without seat belts" among black men gained national attention with the 2000 death of Kansas City linebacker Derrick Thomas, who was fatally injured in a car accident in which his companions were wearing seat belts and he was not.

2

How Black Boys Are Raised

Power is the ability to define reality and have other people respond to your definition as if it were their own.

—JAMAICAN PROVERB

Thomas

I was discussing with a friend of mine who is a father the problems his twelve-year-old son, Thomas, was having after his parents had enrolled him in a nearly all-white junior military academy. My friend said that Thomas hated the school and was being harassed by his classmates who called him "nigger" and "monkey." My friend and his wife are parents firmly ensconced in the black middle class, who have educated their oldest son and daughter in nearly all-white schools from K through 12.

"But Thomas needs to stay there, regardless of what they do to him," his father said to me, as if I had some control over their son's life at the school. "He'll be better able to get into West Point or any other college if he finishes _____ Academy."

"Are you concerned about the psychological damage that is being done to him?" I asked.

"That's a serious charge, and I don't believe that he's undergoing any more pressure there than I faced when I was in school. He's got to learn to adjust to whatever is thrown at him from both blacks and whites."

"Have you talked to the headmaster and teachers at the school?" I asked, knowing that he probably had.

"Sure, that was one of the first things I did, and all of them agreed that the 'transition to a more diverse academy' might come at Tommy's expense."

"You know what I would do"? I asked, ready for opposition to the answer but feeling that my friend was arguing more with himself than with me.

"What?"

"I'd put him in a school where he wouldn't be exposed to such ridicule."

Without hesitation, my friend said, "You're right. I've known this for a long time; I just needed to hear it come from someone else. Why is it so hard to give black boys a good education without all the shit that white people throw on them?" Just like that.

The question my friend asked is the question that most black parents ask at least once during the education of their children. Black parents know that their sons are highly susceptible to circumstances, both unique and not, which render them vulnerable to racist institutions. Black parents possess few strategies, however, that can help them teach their boys how to successfully navigate through these labyrinthine organizations. This should not be interpreted as an indictment of black parenthood, but as an observation that American Africans, in general, and black parents, in particular, have a meager supply of social and educational strategies to protect their sons from a society that has a love-hate relationship with them.

I am still perplexed at how surprised we are when caught

off guard by racism, both overt and covert. We know it exists because not only have we read about it, we've experienced it on a variety of levels and on a daily basis. Yet somehow we still view racism as an aberration rather than a consistent theme in American history. Even educated American Africans (and I use "American Africans" purposely to denote the primacy of Africa in being black in the United States) seem shocked when a close encounter of the racial kind challenges the naive notion that they are somehow immune from it.

In the mid-1990s Tennessee State University—a historically black university located just a few miles from where I used to teach at Fisk University in Nashville—discovered that its students were harassed while leaving football games by the security guards of Nashville's then-new NFL stadium. That a group of black students should be synonymous with "gang presence" was not even the point, but such harassment is commonplace because police *overpatrol* black adolescents, particularly in places such as Daytona Beach during spring break.

I am alternately intrigued and confused by the calls I receive at my office from black parents and educators who are genuinely surprised that at the end of Du Bois's century of race such blatant discrimination is still so commonplace. They are genuinely confounded, fearful, and angry over the vulnerability of their children—particularly their sons—at something so "American" as a college football game. They want to believe that racism is dead, or at least on its deathbed, but, like the masked Jason, it continues to terrorize their children in the most unexpected places and at the most innocuous times.

"Transcending racism" for most American Africans, though viewed cynically by some, is part of the black American dream even though history proves that it will never happen. Derrick Bell's controversial thesis that racism is sewn permanently into the fabric of America is sobering and true. Critical race theorists in law such as Kimberlé Crenshaw provide compelling historical evidence not only that racism is here to stay, but that it mutates itself in ways that ensure its continued survival. American Africans naively remain faithful to strategies and practices that are "mainstream" and thought to be applicable to all people, but that can actually be quite detrimental to some.

One of those practices is child rearing. Very few people—black or white—follow books to the letter on how to raise their children. Instead, they choose to use the information to bolster their knowledge, whether it has been passed on to them or learned firsthand. Indeed, Benjamin Spock's *Baby and Child Care,* one of the bestselling books of all time, serves more as a *manual* rather than a treatise on what to do with children and what to expect at certain ages. It is consulted rather than followed, with the vast majority of parents simply doing what they think best when they raise their children.

Black people in moments of bitter irony can accuse one another—sometimes seriously, sometimes jokingly—of "acting white" or "not acting black enough." William Cross, a noted black psychologist, uses the term *nigrescence* to describe stages of one's psychological identity as an American African. He discusses the Pre-Encounter Stage, during which a black person is oblivious to his/her identity as an African American, while those who incorporate American African culture as essential to their psychological survival belong to the Immersion Stage of nigrescence. Such a model can be applied to black child rearing as well. From my experiences, and based on reams of sociological and psychological research, I believe there are three broad strategies for rearing black children in America: 1) the White Way, 2) the Gray Way, and 3) the Black Way or Warrior Method.

Child–Rearing Strategies

The White Way

The White Way is practiced by most American Africans; it assumes that while society places undue burdens on young black men—police harassment, severe sentencing in juvenile courts, and low expectations for academic performance—it is basically "fair" to them, and if problems do arise, they can be solved within a system that is relatively stable and unbiased. If a black boy gets in trouble at school, it is assumed that, whatever the infraction, the appropriate discipline was meted out fairly and was in the context of the rules governing the school.

Parents who raise their sons in this way come from every class within the American African community. While the method may be identified by the presence of child-rearing books such as Dr. Spock or reading *Parents* magazine in the home, it is also indicated by the total psychological submission of the parents to whatever "system" holds their son. There is little questioning about methods from these parents; in fact, the "system" may be defended, even if its treatment of the black boy is questionable.

While teaching at Fisk University I received a call from a single black mother whose son was complaining about taking Ritalin, a powerful drug that is given disproportionately to young black males. The drug is a stimulant and closely resembles the characteristics of cocaine. Taken orally, it can cause nausea, dizziness, headaches, and severe appetite loss. In 2000, the American Psychiatric Association (APA) was investigated for possible conspiracy with the pharmaceutical giant Ciba-Geigy (now Novartis Pharmaceuticals), the manufacturer of Ritalin, for exaggerating the frequency of attention deficit disorder in order to share in the profit from the drug. By increasing the popularity of this "disorder," the APA increased sales of the drug. The primary takers of Ritalin have been disproportionally boys, and among them it is highly prescribed to black boys.

Her son was given the drug by a psychiatrist when the boy refused to come in from recess, which led to a schoolyard confrontation with his fifth-grade teacher. The boy told his mother that the drug made him "sleepy" (which she better described as "dizzy") and that he was tired of taking it. As a college professor, I had no authority to recommend that the drug be discontinued, but I suggested to the mother that she might want to get a second opinion from another psychiatrist as to whether this medication was necessary.

After a few moments of silence, the mother angrily asked if I *really* cared about her son. I replied that my commitment to the welfare of black children was absolute, and that my recommendation arose from that commitment. "Then how can you tell me not to have the very best drugs for my son?" she said. I told her that Ritalin is often recommended for black boys by educational systems more concerned about controlling them rather than educating them. "You mean to tell me that you think the teacher would recommend something that was not in the best interest of my son?" she asked sarcastically. I told her not only was that possible, but, again, that a trained physician familiar with Ritalin could verify this. In disbelief she said that her son should not have talked back to the teacher and that the teacher had a "right" to control him in any way she could. I paused and gently said that she should have a healthy skepticism about the commitment of any white-run school system that educated her children. Before the words were fully out of my mouth, she'd hung up. I replaced the phone in the cradle, hoping she would take my advice but knowing that she wouldn't.

Is she a "bad" mother? I don't think so. The very fact that she felt compelled to call me shows that she cared a great deal about the welfare of her son. She simply doesn't know how to place his well-being into context within the system to which she is adhering. Moreover, she was actually beholden to a system that has taught *her* that teachers are always right, that doctors know everything, and that schools educate children indiscriminately. She believed that the educational system actually cared about her son and that *he*, not the school, is the problem. Most black parents are convinced that their sons' schools are there to educate them because that is what they have been taught. Though they are more skeptical about the criminal justice system, they remain generally confident that schools are just and impartial in dealing with their sons. Again, this is not an indictment of black parenthood; in fact, it is a description of the misplaced faith that many of them unknowingly place in the institutions surrounding their sons. The White Way of child rearing is unreflective, not because parents of black boys are thoughtless or careless, but because they unconsciously *adjust* to racism's ubiquity and its impact on their children. Racism envelops persons completely and haunts like an unseen ghost in the homes, schools, and workplaces where American Africans live, learn, and work. Noted scholar Lewis Gordon writes in his book *Fanon and the Crisis of European Man* that

With racism's permeation of daily life, grandiose assaults on racism—highly public spectacles against exceptional behavior—miss the mark. Racism, as a function of extraordinary individuals, conceals itself from itself through making its noxious values so familiar and frequent that they cease to function as objects of observation and reflection; they, in short, become unreflective and so steeped in familiarity that they become invisible.

Because I agree with Gordon, I always attempt to objectify to relatives and teachers of black boys the insidious and pernicious nature of white supremacy, and their unwitting acceptance of it within every area of their and their children's lives. I point out that educational curricula glorify the bravery of Patrick Henry but ignore the courage of Ida B. Wells-Barnett. Jefferson is seen as the great American intellectual yet W. E. B. Du Bois is barely discussed in most classrooms. "Classical music" means Bach, Mozart, and Haydn, and ignores the fact that *all* cultures have classical music, including American Africans, who have Scott Joplin, Duke Ellington, and John Coltrane. I challenge them to find one *black* author in *Great Books of the Western World*.

The White Way is not the right way to rear black children and is not selected by black parents as much as it is *accepted*, because of a lack of choice and information and because of the omnipresent nature of racism in the lives of black folk. I know that black parents mean well, because I am a parent myself. We consult friends who offer us well-meaning advice that pertains to raising boys, not *black boys* specifically. We listen to psychologists, teachers, and other experts at parent-teacher meetings give insights on predictable stages of development for boys, *but*

*not specifically black boys. Black boys are not chocolate-covered
white boys.* We browse bookstores and consult manuals that are
not written with our boys in mind: boys who will grow up with
the threat of police harassment, who are watched closely as they
shop in department stores, who are disposed of more harshly by
juvenile justice systems that refer to them as an "endangered
species." We simply cannot all raise our sons the same, because
black boys are different from white boys. Their legacy as American Africans marks them in ways that many whites simply don't
or can't understand.

The Gray Way

The Gray Way of rearing black boys is characterized by parents'
recognizing that the systems through which black boys travel
must be carefully navigated. There is a healthy skepticism about
criticism received from both black and white teachers, who may
not have their sons' best interests at heart. Quite often, black
parents who raise their sons by the Gray Way are viewed as
troublemakers by the institutions that provide services for their
children because they take time to review carefully both sides
of any disciplinary issues. They usually make frequent visits to
the school and write letters to those with authority over their
children, challenging disciplinary action meted out to their sons.

The Gray Way is differentiated from the White Way by a
reaction to racism rather than an unconscious *acceptance* of its
presence. It understands that racism is part of the daily lives of
black people in this country, and shuns solutions that seek to
ignore cultural differences among children. Parents who rear
their children in the Gray Way are often angry and frustrated

at organizations and individuals that seem unrelenting in their denigration of black boys.

An educator and friend of mine recently told the story of how her then-fifteen-year-old son was referred to by his white teacher as "Little Mr. Loser." Not surprisingly, her son was reluctant to go to school after his public humiliation in front of the class. After succeeding in pressing her son to reveal why he was hesitant about returning to his class, she headed straight for his school and angrily told his teacher never to refer to her son in that manner. The teacher sheepishly apologized, and a small victory was gained, only after the mother confronted a teacher who clearly knew a lot about hurting black children and little about nurturing them.

Parents raising their children in the Gray Way are skilled at challenging systems. They know how to organize, write letters, and protest. They may run into conflict with White Way parents who are hesitant at the notion that an institution may need to be challenged so that it ceases its discriminatory behavior toward black boys. They are good parents and spend time listening to their children with a "third ear," as Theodore Reik calls it, which tunes them in to what is happening to their sons. While often disappointed in the unrelenting racism that creates barriers for their sons, they are nonetheless prepared to deal with it, either individually or collectively. They also attempt to support White Way parents, which often proves futile since White Way parents may ridicule them for being too outspoken or simply "too black."

Many Gray Way parents are White Way parents who became convinced that the institutions through which their sons traverse are for white rather than black boys. Their evolution to Grayness comes from believing that institutions do not always do what is in the best interests of black children, particularly black boys. Their social evolution may stop at the Gray Way, or may continue until they begin rearing their sons the Black Way.

The Black Way

One day while volunteering to tell stories to young black children at a local elementary school, I noticed a six-year-old boy pushing a little girl in line in front of him. Scenes like this are repeated thousands of times in elementary schools, but this little girl was not going to put up with it and shoved right back. When I walked over to provide some fatherly discipline, the little boy, clearly frustrated that she was neither impressed nor intimidated by his bullying, called her a "ho." I was shocked to hear the word coming from his six-year-old lips but, sadly, not surprised. He saw me right after he said it, and looked sheepishly down at the floor. I asked him where he'd heard the word, and he quietly answered "TV." "What does it mean?" I asked; he answered that it was a "girl who did something bad." I told him to apologize, and he did, turning only slightly to the frowning young lady who had now crossed her little arms and was glaring at him. I then motioned for him to follow me out of the line and into a corner, where I spent the next twenty minutes giving him simple lessons in courtesy.

About a half hour later, my new little friend, who was by now telling me the things six-year-olds tell adults, asked if he could sit on my lap during storytime. I told him yes, since I was at the school being a "role model" for the children. He then looked at me quizzically and asked in the sincerest of voices, "You my daddy?" I was touched by this simple question. I quietly answered that I was like a father to him, as well as to all the other children there. This was all he needed to hear, and he instantly announced to his friends gathering at the table, "He my daddy!" and although they laughed, they did not dispute his claim. He then hugged me tightly, and we began to read a story together.

I thought it telling that this child, who was now seeking fatherly acceptance and guidance, had only a moment before been acting out what he'd come to believe—even at his tender age—was his role in regards to his young sister. A victim of various media's pernicious effect on young black boys, this six-year-old boy was already adept in how to denigrate girls. By the time he grows to adulthood, he'll be even better skilled at disrespecting black women. The way we raise our black boys in America has been a poor imitation of the way white boys are raised. Those who raise black boys are, with few exceptions, ignoring the impact of racism on our children and are casual about teaching black boys the importance of understanding and respecting other American Africans. The misguided but popular notion that it takes grit to succeed in school is a not-so-subtle way of placing the onus for children's educational success entirely on their shoulders and avoids the much-needed discussion of how racism impacts the educational success of black children. Black Way parents are rare. At the core of their child-rearing methods is the belief that African-centered methods and values are the *only* choice in raising healthy black boys in America. The celebration of African culture is reflected in their homes with artwork, books, and memorabilia reflecting a love of Africa. Kwanzaa is given a place in their homes, and its *Nguzo Saba* (Seven Principles) are valued throughout the year and taught to future generations.

These parents see their sons as warriors and *Jegnas* doing battle on several levels with racism, and they support them in these

struggles. While their sons may go to traditionally white institutions for education or recreation, they believe that, at best, these
institutions can *train* their children but not *educate* them. They
believe their children's education is the direct responsibility of
parents and relatives, and they know that their children's education goes far beyond the four walls of a school. They see black
institutions such as African-centered churches, museums, and
universities as bastions against traditional methods of learning,
and place their sons in environments where they can learn about
self as well as things.

Similar to Gray Way parents, Black Way parents find protest
a necessary tool to ensure that their sons will receive proper
treatment in whatever organization they find membership.
Their protest, however, is made with the idea of *systemic* change
that will challenge the very essence of the organization. These
changes can take the form of creating an alternative school,
college, or recreational group that is more culturally specific
to African ideals. The education of their children is viewed as
belonging to the parents and not the school system, and care is
taken in who educates their children as well as where they are
educated. When their sons reach university level, historically
black colleges and universities are high on their list; even if the
final college selection is a traditionally white institution, their
sons are carefully guided and counseled on the major selection
with regard to professors' attitudes toward black boys.

Black Way parents tirelessly recruit from the ranks of White
Way and Gray Way parents, by introducing to them African-
centered values in the form of institutions, books, celebrations,
dress, and food. They may invite other parents to the increasingly popular "rites of passage" ceremonies for black boys, which
induct them into manhood. Black Way parents focus on insti-

tutional change and, again, while protest is in their repertoire, it is viewed as a means to an end rather than an end in itself. They see an African inside of every "Negro," and they encourage his emergence in conversation. They believe that the adoption of African-centered values is transformational and not just a ceremonial exercise employing African clothing and hairstyles. The transformation goes far deeper into cherishing values that reflect the strength and courage of long-forgotten ancestors who triumphed in the face of adversity.

The Warrior Method of Raising Black Boys

I chose colors to introduce these three ways of raising black males in order to create a visual image of how racism impacts upon the rearing of our children. The "Black Way," however, is better referred to as the Warrior Method, since it implies that those who are serious about the healthy passage of black males from boyhood to manhood must *fight* to accomplish this. I use the word *fight* because it is exactly that.

Educators of black boys, whatever their race, if dedicated to the unpopular proposition that they wish to have a healthy, safe, and relaxed environment for black boys, will be challenged in their efforts to accomplish this. Teachers who adopt the Warrior Method often run headlong into trouble at the schools in which they teach. Yaa Asantewaa Nzingha, a middle school teacher in Brooklyn, was absent from her drama class for one day. Richard Levine taught the twenty-five-year veteran schoolteacher's class in her absence and asked her students to do some improvisational acting. He asked one of the students to pretend that he was stealing something as a way of impressing girls. The student said no because "all black people don't steal." When Levine asked the young Kurtis Lee who taught him that, Lee responded, "Ms. Nzingha teaches us that as Africans we shouldn't fall into the standards of America." Nzingha was placed under investigation for telling her students that they are *not* Americans but Africans. Efforts were made to suspend this teacher, who has won extraordinary praise from the very system that investigated her, and to revoke her New York teaching license as well. Her African-centered curriculum, taught at a school that supposedly encourages individual expression, runs squarely in the face of administrators who are resentful toward Warrior Method teachers who want the best for their students. In late 2000, she was fired from the Brooklyn, New York, school system and, as of this writing, is banned from teaching in the State of New York because of her protest. In 2015, Marilyn Zuniga was fired for responding to a request by her students to write get-well letters to political prisoner Mumia Abu-Jamal, who was wrongfully convicted of killing a police officer in 1981. She thought the students' request showed civic understanding, compassion for imprisoned people, and was a humane gesture coming from her third-grade students. Zuniga's and her students' actions were met with a firestorm of protest from police unions and the school board, who fired her. She is currently suing the Orange, New Jersey, school board for wrongful termination.

White persons in particular will be queried closely about why they are "going to the mats" for a black male in ways that are subtly racist. This may seem harsh, but many well-meaning whites view working with black boys as "missionary work." Black boys do not need saviors, they need advocates who will aid in their healthy development. The popular theme of white people saving black males is portrayed in such films as *Sunset Park, Dangerous Minds* (an interesting title), and *Class Act.* Hollywood enjoys the plot of white persons rescuing black people from a host of evils, perhaps as a way of obtaining absolution from past evils toward them. They may be viewed by other whites as a "traitor" to the idea that black boys are part of a throwaway generation, who do not deserve the attention they receive from their white intercessors.

Black intercessors willing to adopt the Warrior Method will also face stiff opposition as they defy systems and procedures that hurt black boys. They may force a school system to enhance the celebration of Black History Month, agitate for the inclusion of black heroes and sheroes on the walls gazed upon by young black males who rarely see blacks in positive adult roles. The Warrior Method calls for a vigilance toward media, schools, churches, and social-service agencies that serve black boys. The Warrior Method provides appropriate reading lists, has ready a set of lawyers who argue for justice under the law, and is aware of cultural events that will enhance the self-esteem of black boys. This method calls for a full-time commitment to do battle with systems that are oblivious to the needs of black boys. The Warrior method is not a battle that will be enjoined only by black people, but by anyone serious about eliminating social barriers that block the paths toward healthy development in young black boys.

Very few people have a clear understanding of the challenges faced by black boys as they mature. We already know that there is denial in America about the entrenched nature of racism, as demonstrated in polls taken shortly after the Charlottesville white supremacist march in August 2017. A Gallup poll reported that 61 percent of Americans believed antiblack racism in the

United States was a major problem compared to the 51 percent who said this at the beginning of the Obama presidency in 2009. The caveat is that this 61 percent is split along racial lines: 82 percent of American Africans feel this way and only 56 percent of whites. A Quinnipiac poll found something even more disturbing: 66 percent of nonwhite people labeled racism a "very serious" problem while only 39 percent of whites felt this; 25 percent of whites said it was not a serious problem at all while only 11 percent of nonwhites felt that way. Recent polls taken since the ascendency of Donald Trump to become the president of the United States indicates that this denial of racism in contemporary America has reached epidemic proportions. In a 2017 poll conducted by National Public Radio, the Robert Wood Johnson Foundation, and the Harvard T. H. Chan School of Public Health shows that 55 percent of white Americans believe that racism is directed toward them and that blacks exaggerate how racism occurs in police encounters. A consistent finding in several national surveys is that there is an ever-widening gulf between blacks and whites on a number of social issues that range from affirmative action to the presence of racial prejudice and job opportunity. These differences are increasing rather than decreasing, and they destroy the notion that in times of prosperity racism will disappear like dew when met with the sun's rays. If dedicated people who raise, teach, work with, and volunteer for black boys are up to these challenges, they will commit in tangible ways to the children they work with. Magical solutions that many parents and educators are looking for when working with black males don't exist. There are no easy ways to counter the assaults aimed at black boys. The ten points that follow are what I consider essential in beginning an effective intervention with black boys. They come from listening to parents and educators over many years as well as putting them into practice in my own teaching. More will be said about this in chapter 4.

The Ten Commitments of the Warrior Method

1. *Maintain a strong commitment to educating black boys.* Too often just lip service is paid to working with black boys. Rather, consultants should be brought in to give workshops and provide recommendations for challenges facing educators and human service workers. Educators who claim they want the best for black boys should know about them, read about them, play with them, and, most of all, intervene on their behalf if they are unjustly punished for minor infractions.

2. *Possess a deep and abiding knowledge of global black history.* No parent or educator of children should be unaware of the history of the children they teach. The Kenyan proverb "Until lions have historians, hunters will be heroes" is vital when educating black boys; it emphasizes the importance of reversing perspectives in telling the history of black people. I have seen the eyes of black children light up when they hear about Nzingah's courage against the Portuguese, Wells-Barnett's commitment to justice, and Denmark Vesey's dedication to freedom. A committed educator will use these stories to help black boys locate themselves psychologically in the river of black history. See the annotated bibliography for books about black history.

The idea of Africans in the *Maafa na Maangamizi* possessing an African-centered worldview did not begin with the Afrocentric movement in the mid-1970s. It has been a consistent theme throughout the writings of black people in all parts of the world. In this country, Maria Stewart (1803–1879) of Boston, the first American African woman to publish her speeches, refused to let anyone address her as other than "an African." Throughout her life she remained outspoken about the "need of Africans to build their own schools and stores." Her book, *Meditations from the Pen of Mrs. Maria Stewart*, was written totally from the perspective of being an African in America rather than an "African American." Likewise, David Walker's (circa 1785–1830) *Appeal to the Colored Citizens of the World,* written in 1829, called for self-defense among all enslaved Africans and stated that "it is no more harm for you to kill the man who is trying to kill you than it is for you to take a drink of water." Martin Delany (1812–1885), a physician and the highest-ranking black person in the Union Army, signed a contract with the Nigerian government in 1859 that allowed for cotton production by free West Africans and serious negotiations to repatriate all Africans in the *Maafa na Maangamizi* back to their Motherland.

Such calls for an African-centered consciousness persisted in this country during the twentieth century with the Harlem Renaissance and abroad during the 1920s with the *Négritude* movement and West Africans such as Aimé Césaire, Leon Dumas, and Leopold Senghor. Perhaps the greatest manifestation of this African-centered consciousness was the efforts of Marcus Garvey's Back to Africa movement, which mobilized millions of Africans in the United States, the

Caribbean, and Europe to look toward Africa as a place for freedom and true liberation. His influence can be found in the writings of Elijah Muhammad (1897–1975) of the Nation of Islam. W. E. B. Du Bois (1868–1963), the "father of pan-Africanism," would also discuss the importance of being an African, would spend his last years in Ghana and eventually die and be buried there. Audley Moore (1898–1997), better known as "Queen Mother Moore," would become one of the greatest proponents of African-centered education of this century and would consistently be listed with Elijah Muhammad and Marcus Garvey as one of the greatest organizers of American Africans during the twentieth century.

3. *Read at least thirty minutes a day on African/African American culture and life.* Similar to the second commitment, the dedicated mentors to black boys will learn more about the culture from which they emerge. They will read books and magazines that will teach them about what black boys are seeing, hearing, and talking about. I am surprised about how little black parents know about hip-hop culture, thereby cutting off an avenue of communication with their sons. Asking a black boy what he learned in school will get far less attention than asking him if he has heard a particular Dead Prez album. Parents and educators, without using gimmicks, should use "bridges" to reach the black boys with whom they are familiar. Communicating with black boys about their thoughts, music, and heroes begins the process of socializing them in productive ways.

4. *Be comfortable in predominantly black environments.* I always ask white teachers if they feel comfortable in black

churches, universities, and other social settings where they
are a minority. Many white people find it difficult to exist
in such surroundings since they may feel more comfortable controlling their environment than learning from it.
A preacher friend of mine says, "White people don't make
good minorities." Funny though this may be, the truth is that
most white people spend very little time immersed in black
surroundings. The converse is true, and black people are
encouraged to "adjust" to their predominantly white settings,
be it a school, the workplace, or the location of leisure-time
activity. It is not uncommon for black parents to tell me that
they chose to send their children to a predominantly white
college so that they "can get used to dealing with white folks,"
as if this would not happen as a matter of course as their children mature. Most whites, however, are not prepared for predominantly black environments; they actually go out of their
way to avoid them. Those interested in adopting the Warrior
Method in raising or teaching black boys must acknowledge
and lose such inhibitions if they wish to operate sincerely in
their interactions with them.

5. *Attend African-centered religious institutions.* The faith
   community remains a powerful influence in black communities. It serves as an excellent bridge for helping the spiritual
   growth of American African boys, and is a place for organizing
   around issues affecting them. I am impressed with teachers
   who participate in black spiritual gatherings and are aware of
   how black churches can help in working with black boys. It is
   important to remember, however, that *attendance* alone at a
   faith-based institution does not make one a "good" Christian,
   Muslim, Jew, Buddhist, or Hindu, no more than going to

McDonald's makes one a hamburger. Black churches with white images of Jesus are poisonous to the psychological well-being of black people, especially our children. Period. Our spiritual expression should be an outgrowth of our cultural heritage and a white Jesus is simply alien to it.

6. *Volunteer at least five hours a month in a human service activity that engages black boys.* The emphasis here again is to know the environments in which black boys learn and play. Volunteering is an indication of commitment to addressing the needs of black boys. Serving as a teacher's aide, coaching basketball, and attending meetings at Boys and Girls Clubs can give volunteers a more comprehensive view of black boys' lives in America.

7. *Understand all bureaucracies that impact black boys.* This is a major task but necessary in committing to working with and raising black boys. I encourage parents, teachers, and volunteers who work with black boys to know who serves on the governing boards of institutions they attend, and who directs, administers, and otherwise runs the organizations. They should be familiar with the annual reports, should discuss "insider information" about the diversity of the administrators on the board, and should know who funds the organization and how much is being donated to it. Who is the chief of police? Who is the clerk in the juvenile court? Who makes up the health care organizations that are sensitive to pediatric care of black boys? Information of this nature should be readily available to persons interested in black boys in case strategic protest becomes necessary in advocating for them.

8. *Organize against environments oppressive of black boys.*
Those committed to ensuring the healthy development of
black boys should be prepared to intervene politically on
their behalf. Protest against policies or individuals who exercise discriminatory behavior toward black boys should be a
tactic in the arsenal of those who adopt the Warrior Method
of raising them.

9. *Read the following five books:*
Beloved by Toni Morrison—The greatest American African
love story ever told. It details the emotional impact of
slavery on Africans in America. Based on the true story of
Margaret Garner, who, in 1856, slashed the throat of one
of her children rather than have them returned to slavery,
the book tells about the impact of enslavement on the
relationships between black women and men.

Yurugu by Marimba Ani—Perhaps the most comprehensive African-centered critique of European systems of
thought ever written. Ani makes the necessary connections between how European systems by design support
discriminatory behavior toward people of color.

The Miseducation of the Negro by Carter G. Woodson—The
classic book offered by the "father" of American African
history, on why blacks *and* whites have been miseducated.
Written over eighty years ago, it gives the reader a comprehensive view of how to educate black people.

The Isis Papers by Frances Cress Welsing—Welsing's thesis
on the global system of white supremacy is still unchallenged. A most important book to read. In clear language
she tells how the system of white supremacy works and
what to do about it.

The New Jim Crow: Mass Incarceration in the Age of Colorblindness by Michelle Alexander—The issue of crime and black males is almost always taken out of historical context. Alexander's book traces the historical pattern of confining black men to enslavement, convict labor, and now mass incarceration.

10. *Teach at least two other persons each month about the Ten Commitments.* At every opportunity, educators and parents should provide counterpoints to the negative stereotyping of black boys. Discussing these commitments is a small but necessary step in dismantling these stereotypes.

The Ten Commitments are tough assignments, but successfully raising black boys in a racist society is a difficult job. I know, because I am constantly bombarded with questions from the private, public, and educational sectors on how to raise/teach/educate/entertain/discipline/talk to/impress/cajole/understand black boys by persons who, though sincere, are looking for a quick fix that simply does not exist. Questions are rarely asked about the "challenges of raising white girls." White boys, until recently, were thought to be fairly well integrated into "mainstream" America. Witness the orgies in Daytona Beach during spring break: higher levels of anxiety were raised in response to the black gatherings than to the white gatherings even though both were far less destructive than what has occurred in that city for years. "Boys will be boys" may be more accurately stated as "white boys will be white boys"; black boys don't "enjoy the privilege" of raucous behavior to the same extent as their white counterparts.

Chester Himes once said, "Martyrs are needed to create incidents. Incidents are needed to create revolutions. Revolutions are needed to create progress." Black boys live in a world that has strong and misguided opinions about them, based on centuries of misinformation. It will take sometimes abrasive strategies to effect the changes necessary to guarantee them a fair chance at life. Those who are committed to them need to be prepared with strategies that include both negotiation and confrontation that will lead to revolution.

3

Barack Obama, and Other Victims of White Supremacy

On Being a Victim of White Supremacy

Black people misunderstand and misuse the term *victim* because the system of white supremacy (S.O.W.S.) equates "being a victim" with helplessness. Rosa Parks was a victim of white supremacy and so was Martin Luther King and Malcolm X, yet they were far from "helpless." *Victim* is a term co-opted by the S.O.W.S. which makes us afraid to use it in our discourses about white supremacy. In most instances, black folk misuse the term *victim* because they have drunk the Kool-Aid of the white supremacists and let them define it for them. Oddly enough, people do not have trouble describing themselves as a victim of a natural disaster such as a hurricane, flood, or forest fire. In these instances, they will proudly assert that although they are victims of these disasters, they will "rebuild," "carry on," and "stay put." They see themselves as resilient, tough, and assertive, and in spite of the natural disaster that has befallen them they will "hang in there and save the tradition of the community."

A few years ago, Harry Allen, former "media assassin" of the seminal hip-hop group Public Enemy, wrote what I consider the best analysis of being a "victim of white supremacy" and sets the record straight on what victimhood really means.

If I walked down Fifth Avenue, in New York, and a white man punched me in my jaw, and knocked me down, I would be the victim of a punch.

If I fell to the ground, I would still be the victim of a punch. If I, in response, sat on the curb and began to cry, I would still be the victim of a punch.

If, in response, I absorbed the blow, but kept walking down Fifth Avenue, I would still be the victim of a punch.

If, in response, I fell to the ground, got up, and knocked the white man who punched me down with a punch, I would still be the victim of a punch.

If, in response, I fell to the ground, got up, pulled out a Tec-9, and began to fire wildly at him and every white person on the street, killing dozens of white people, I would still be the victim of a punch.

If, in response, I fell to the ground, got up, pulled out a Tec-9, and began to fire wildly at him and every white person on the street, killing dozens of white people, except one wounded white woman, upon whom I had compassion, taking her home, nursing her back to health, and marrying her, I would still be the victim of a punch.

And if, after years of happy life together, I should die, I would still be the victim of a punch.

Many people attempt to equate victim status with the

then-presumed inability of a victim to compensate for victimization, e.g., 'I'm not a victim. I'm a survivor.'

To which I say, 'Well, what is it that you are surviving?' Answer: 'Your victimization.' As though 'victim' and 'survivor' were inevitably two different things. (And maybe, ultimately, they are. But is there any black person whom, in the same manner, could describe himself or herself as 'a survivor of racism'?)

These people equate 'victim' with 'powerless' victim.

The two are not necessarily the same.

The latter may, in fact, not exist.

Barack Obama was a victim of white supremacy, as are all nonwhite people, because he was constrained by the S.O.W.S. in what he could say or do, especially when he discussed race and racism. The system does not allow its victims to speak freely and honestly about racism, and when a victim does, the response is swift and decisive. What follows are my thoughts as to why many of the events of the Obama presidency are better understood in the context of a white supremacist society that morphs events that are clearly racist into more palatable explanations for people classified as white.

A Conference Call About "Change"

My phone rang steadily the night of November 4, 2008. Friends, family, and colleagues called me from around the world to describe their feelings about what had just happened: a black man had just won the presidency of the United States. In those surreal minutes between the phone calls, I had several feelings:

joy, fear, apprehension, doubt, anger, and anxiety. Eerily, they matched the feelings of the folks who called me, especially those of fear and anxiety. These two emotions fell into two categories: fear that he would be assassinated, and anxiety about what he could accomplish as president of a white supremacist nation. My more cynical friends saw him as a tool of white supremacy and emphasized the fact that he had become president of the United States and at best would only carry out the same policies as his forty-three predecessors, especially as it pertained to Africans in America.

The fear in my friends and me coalesced when Barack, Michelle, Sasha, and Malia walked out on the stage of Grant Park in Chicago before 240,000 people. On one hastily convened conference call, everyone expressed worries that he would be shot in front of the crowd and his presidency would end before it began. One of my friends openly wept over the phone and asked the rhetorical question, "Why is he standing out there like that?! Where is his Secret Service protection?!" It was in that moment I realized that all of us on the phone understood without even saying it out loud that this nation had four hundred years of killing, defaming, exiling, and assassinating black people who disrupted its commitment to expanding and refining white supremacy.

After projecting what had happened to Harriet, Ida, Rosa, Malcolm, and Martin onto Barack, we began to talk about whether or not he could or would "make a difference" to black people. We fantasized about reparations, Supreme Court judges, and stronger economic ties to Africa while the cynics on the line said that none of this would happen because he would be constrained by the system of white supremacy. One of my closest friends asked, "Do you really think that white folks are going to let a black man change Babylon?" Some of us said, "We'll see."

Some of us said, "I don't know." Some of us said, "No." Some of us said, "Hell, no." But only one person said, "Yes," and it wasn't me. I expressed a "wait and see" attitude, but my doubts about "change" coming to America rose from our best teacher, history.

The Cold, the Cannons, and the Screams

I wanted to go to the Inauguration, and between Obama's Chicago speech and January 20, 2009, the only other time I recall black people talking more about racism and politics was during the 1960s and 1970s. Barbers, store clerks, Christians, Muslims, atheists, educators, mail carriers, the homeless, and the homebound shared their authoritative opinions about President-Elect Barack Obama. "Everyone," of course, had voted for him, just like every black man after the 1995 Million Man March swore they had been there even though I knew many had not. Like on election night, I heard elders from my generation say, "They are going to kill him like they did King and Kennedy," but from students I heard much more optimism about his upcoming presidency. From both groups, I heard praise that he had married a "real sister" and that he wasn't an "Uncle Tom" like Herman Cain, the failed black Republican who had been promptly eliminated in that party's primaries. Like many others, I listened to candidate Obama's speech on racism in America in March 2008, and was quite surprised at his skill at unraveling, examining, and explaining the tangled threads of white supremacy that were sewn into the fabric of this nation from its birth. However, like so many other black men before him, he had been forced to "publicly repudiate" the remarks made in what America deemed "racist" language when used by an assertive

black person. Obama's pastor, Dr. Jeremiah Wright, one of the
most progressive black ministers in this country, telling the truth
about this nation's damnable actions toward black people was
considered unacceptable in a nation that always saw outspoken
and unbought black people as a threat to the S.O.W.S. For me,
throwing Dr. Wright under the bus in order to appease a ner-
vous white America about his candidacy was the first indication
Obama would capitulate on using the bully pulpit to speak publicly about racism to a country that never had.

I did two things in the week before the Inauguration that
would become symbolic of my attitude toward President Obama.
I bought a "bubble coat," thick with lining that would make
anyone sweat in a Siberian winter, and I purchased a new state-
of-the-art digital camera that would ensure I would capture the
historic day as clearly as possible. After two winters, the coat
became dysfunctional because of a faulty zipper. My "bubble"
burst about "change in America." I also dropped the camera and
couldn't see a thing out of it except dark shadows—to me symbolic of how racism would be the ghost haunting anything this
nation would do with its darker people.

When I arrived at the National Mall, it was cold. The wind
was blowing pretty hard and hundreds of thousands of people
were there. One could easily be seduced that the crowd represented the "goodness of America," the "rainbow coalition" that
Jesse Jackson talked about, or the "workers united" that my
Marxist friends opined about. For me, it represented something
far simpler—we all just wanted to be there to witness a historical
moment that most of us thought was impossible given the racism
in this land mass. As I look back, I wanted to make sure that I
could give an eyewitness account to my grandchildren of what I

experienced that day, so I took dozens of pictures with my soon-to-be-broken Nikon camera inside of my very warm bubble coat.

I stood to the left of the stage about 150 yards away from the podium and had crosstalk conversations with everyone around me. Everyone was smiling and conversed about hope, change, and tomorrows. I listened and talked as well and asked a lot of "what about . . ." questions to anyone who would listen, and friendly debates popped up all over as the clock moved toward noon—something the writers of the Constitution inserted as the mandatory time a new president had to be sworn in. After Chief Justice Roberts completely mangled the oath, I, like other black people around me, wondered if it was a deliberate act in what turned out to be the first in a series of attempts to delegit-imize Barack Obama's presidency. His white supremacist suc-cessor, Donald John Trump, would launch his presidential bid by using this tactic, succeed at it, and then proceed to have the most laughable and dangerous presidency in American history. I heard a comedian once say that Donald Trump is the presi-dent that white supremacists thought Barack Obama would be. I agree. . . .

A few minutes after Aretha sang "America the Beautiful" in a crown that was even more beautiful and Joseph Lowery prayed a prayer for the ages, the crowd began to disperse. Suddenly, just a few yards from where we stood, a twenty-one-gun salute rang out and people screamed. I immediately thought that someone had set off a bomb. We were that close to the guns and I ducked like the people around me. Some people began to run and I braced for what I imagined would be next. Almost immediately, someone yelled, "It's just a twenty-one-gun salute!" and people who only a few seconds ago were scared out of their wits laughed uneasily about the noise and their misguided panic. It wasn't a bomb, of course, but our reactions to the shots expressed the primeval memory common to American Africans who associate guns and screams with violence toward our leaders. It also foreshadowed the political and racist explosions that would occur throughout the young president's first and second term.

Break–Ins and Beer

On July 22, 2009, I knew that Barack Obama was just another black man and a victim of the system of white supremacy. Henry Louis Gates, a faculty member at Harvard University, had mistakenly been arrested by the Cambridge, Massachusetts, police for climbing through a window after he was unable to open the front door of his own house. His arrest sparked a national debate on racial profiling—something black people in this country talk about all the time and whites seemed oblivious to—and the conversation extended itself to the White House. Here's how the question was asked by a journalist and answered by President Obama:

> Lynn Sweet, a reporter for the *Chicago Sun-Times*: Recently, Professor Henry Louis Gates Jr. was arrested at his home in Cambridge. What does that incident say to you? And what does it say about race relations in America?

> President Obama: Now, I've—I don't know, not having been there and not seeing all the facts, what role race played in that. But I think it's fair to say, number one, any of us would be pretty angry; number two, that the

Cambridge police acted stupidly in arresting somebody
when there was already proof that they were in their own
home. And number three, what I think we know separate
and apart from this incident is that there is a long history
in this country of African-Americans and Latinos being
stopped by law enforcement disproportionately. That's
just a fact.

It was a cringeworthy moment and I knew immediately that
his condemnation of the Cambridge police by calling them "stupid" would cause a firestorm. It did. One Fraternal Order of
Police president disingenuously accused Obama of damaging
relations between the police and the community, as if they were
not damaged already. Massachusetts police unions collectively
demanded an apology not only from President Obama, but from
Deval Patrick, the black governor of the state. Thaddeus McCot-
ter, a Republican congressman from Michigan, introduced a res-
olution in the House calling for an apology by President Obama
to James Crowley, the arresting officer in the case. A Pew poll
that was conducted showed that white voter support dropped
overnight from 53 to 46 percent.

Two days later, and again from the White House, President
Obama meekly apologized to the Cambridge Police Department and Crowley. He said that his words "could have [been]
calibrated . . . differently," and, similar to what he had done with
Dr. Wright, threw Gates (only partially) under the bus by saying
that "Professor Gates probably overreacted as well." He called
both Gates and Crowley and invited them to what eventually
would be called the "beer summit" at the White House to "bring
people together" on the thorny issue of racism. I understand
the optics of such meetings, but I shook my head as I saw yet

another powerful but "uppity" black man castrated in public by the American public. During the six months prior to that fateful press conference, President Obama had held twenty meetings with the press; in the next six months, he held only six. . . .

President Barack Obama's public lynching began that day and continued with shouts of "You lie!" during a State of the Union Address, racist cartoons circulating over thousands of computers across America the beautiful, white governors shaking their fingers in his face, and Donald Trump launching his political future on "birtherism." His public lynching, though symbolic, placed him in the same circle of death with Michael Brown, Laquan McDonald, Trayvon Martin, Alton Sterling, and Tamir Rice. The American bullet had killed them just as the American hand choked the life out of Eric Garner and tightened its grip on Obama's presidency. It was difficult for me to separate the police murders of black boys and men that were recorded, broadcasted, and televised globally from what was happening to the president. In 2013, when vigilante George Zimmerman was found not guilty for killing Trayvon Martin and President Obama opined, "You know, when Trayvon Martin was first shot I said that this could have been my son. Another way of saying that is: Trayvon Martin could have been me thirty-five years ago," the nation went apoplectic. Talking heads deemed it "inappropriate," and claimed that the president was just being the "race-baiter in chief." The country did not want to hear a black Barack Obama connect himself racially with a black boy. They preferred him deracinated, "mixed," and "half black and half white" if you please, but never really "black." After all, didn't "liberal" Senate Majority Leader Harry Reid, during Obama's first run for the presidency, say that the country was ready to embrace a black man as president because he was "light-skinned," had "oratorical skills," and was without a "Negro dialect, unless he wanted to have one"?

I believe the black man who lived at 1600 Pennsylvania Avenue, Washington, DC 20500, was no different than Philando Castile, who was shot in cold blood by a police officer in Minnesota. Both did what they were supposed to do under trying circumstances. Both lived in nice neighborhoods. Both were obeying the law. Both had beautiful families and small children. Both were loved by the communities from which they emerged. Both were seen as threatening to brainwashed people who saw black men as subhumans, and ultimately both were killed—one literally and the other politically. In years to come, the Obama presidency will be analyzed ad infinitum, and I think that one day this country will be brave enough to say that white supremacy was the most important but neglected factor in determining much of what happened during his administration. If that day comes, I hope that same factor will be included in understanding why black men suffer mass incarceration, poverty, unemployment, substandard education, and disproportionate killing by police officers and premature death. The following chapters will present a method that can ensure the healthy development of black males who wish to challenge a system that daily forces them to compromise their African selves.

4

Necessary Tools for African Warriors

The present system under the control of the whites trains the Negro to be white and at the same time convinces him of the impropriety of the impossibility of his becoming white. It compels the Negro to become a good Negro for the performance of which his education is ill-suited. —CARTER G. WOODSON

NWA

I was waiting in the cluttered office of the diminutive-looking white teacher, observing the drawings and desk that most middle school teachers have. Her disheveled appearance matched her office, and I glanced at a small plant that was begging to be watered on a bookshelf. The shelf was populated with volumes about inner-city life with yellow stickies protruding from them. The teacher had asked me months earlier to speak to her class—a group of about fifteen black boys, who for one reason or another had failed to learn the school curriculum. She was now down the corridor on "hall duty," monitoring the students to make sure they got to their classes without incident. I took the moment alone to glimpse at the memorabilia teachers display when their students do well on their assignments. There were holiday essays about the self-effacing pilgrims, Columbus's meanderings throughout the West Indies, and the greatness of Washington and Jefferson. Not one symbol in the teacher's office was culturally specific to the children she was assigned to teach. As I continued my visual tour of her office, I was interrupted by her entering the room and apologizing for making me wait. Out of breath and clearly frazzled, she began to describe the students to whom I was about to speak. They were "very unruly," she said, and had a near-total disregard for "authority." She gave me an advance apology for their behavior and said that she saw the importance of "black men as role models for young black boys," and that this was her motivation in asking me to speak to them during Black History Month.

I nodded my head, having been part of this scene so many times. I'd even mused on the idea of creating a for-profit agency dubbed Rent a Middle-class Brother for your Organization (RAMBO); requests for such engagements are very frequent and involve black men from the business, educational, and government sectors. The teacher was rambling on distractedly about how all the boys "defied" authority and how she simply had "no idea" about how to "control them." I was sure that I would talk to them about self-esteem; how I would begin I did not know, but I was eager to get started and steered her to the door. Before entering the classroom, she gave me one last apologetic look, as if she were leading me before a firing squad.

The chaotic class was filled with about fifteen black boys between the ages of twelve and fourteen who were engaged in everything from cursing to playing cards. Two sat in the back completely zoned out, the music from their earphones audible over the din. The others, talking loudly about girls and other things, totally disregarded our presence. Their teacher almost crept into the room ahead of me. Once inside she asked everyone to take a seat "because there was a guest speaker." Several of the boys continued talking as they slowly complied with her directions and sat down. We both knew that her waiting for absolute silence would be a waste of time, so she began *reading* the introduction I had provided her with while the boys continued their discussion about things more important to them. In fact, their voices grew louder as she droned on.

When she said my name, signaling the end of her soliloquy, I got up in front of the class and said good morning. A few replied, but most were indifferent or simply ignored me altogether. On impulse, I turned to the blackboard and wrote in the largest letters possible "NWA." I then asked what the letters stood for, and nearly all the boys said, "Niggas with Attitude." I had done the first thing that any teacher needs to do: get the students' attention. I next asked them why a group of young black men would call themselves "niggas." Nearly all the boys replied that it was a term of endearment and that it was not negative unless a *white* person called them that. I told them that I thought it was negative, and they all disagreed. I had done the second thing that a teacher needed to do: engage them in a dialogue.

I then asked how many of them cared if I called them "nigga." When no one replied, I said that for the next ten minutes I would do exactly that. They laughed and challenged me to go ahead. I started asking them questions about what words like *self-esteem, success,* and *challenges* meant, and I made sure that, regardless of who answered my question, I would preface it by saying, "Yes, Nigga," when I called on him. I continued to call them "nigga" throughout each exchange, and ended by saying, "Thanks, Nigga." After about five minutes, it was clear that I was causing unease with my casual use of the word. Their laughter had long faded, and the boys were becoming agitated and angry. Suddenly, one of the students raised his hand; after I acknowledged him by saying, "Yes, Nigga," he replied that he did not like my calling him that. I asked why, and he said that it sounded different the way I was using it. I asked how, and he said it just didn't sound the same and that it seemed so ugly now that I had drawn his attention to it. His classmates nodded in agreement. I thanked him without calling him a "nigga," then explained what the words *objectification* and *brainwashing* meant. The third and most important task of a teacher had taken place: the students had rolled an idea around in their heads, considered it, and *learned* something.

I launched into a brief discussion about how black people could remake different words that reflected self-esteem, as had occurred with *black* during the 1960s and *African* during the 1990s. I went on to explain that the word *Nigga* was only *rented* and not *owned* by us, and that was the reason why we felt it was a term that only we could use to describe ourselves or one another. One of the boys asked me if a white person had ever called me a "nigga." I said yes, several times, and that the time I remembered most was from when I was twelve and was feeding my dogs in the backyard of our Hough Avenue house in Cleveland. Some southern white men, who had managed to come north and were camping in the parking lot of a soon-to-be-all-black bar named Jo-Lu's, next door to where we lived, called me a "nigger" for no other reason than intimidation. I said nothing, fed my dogs, went inside, and told my father what had happened. Without even getting the details, he went down in the basement, retrieved a baseball bat, and told me to come with him. I obeyed and walked into the backyard with him. When he

saw the men, he asked me which one called me that. I pointed
to him. By this time the displaced southerners started backing
up even though they outnumbered my father six to one. He ran
toward the man who was halfway up a chain-link fence that bor-
dered the yard. The other men scattered, and my father told the
one on the fence that if he ever saw him again he would "kick
his ass." I felt good. So did the boys in the classroom. They were
listening to my story with rapt attention, and I ended by telling
them it was important for black fathers to protect their sons.

For the next thirty minutes, learning took place in the classroom. We talked about the importance of education and knowledge of black culture and history. We discussed the importance
of reading something every day about black people's contribu-
tion to world culture and American society. We talked about
the importance of educating other black boys about how society
hurts them both physically and psychologically. We finished by
discussing the need for excellence in whatever they did as black
boys. I then told them that they were young warriors in a battle
to retain and understand who they are as young black people
and that they must never compromise the part of them that
was African. I listened and became overwhelmed by how all of
these handsome young black boys were eager to learn, eager
to contribute, but were understimulated by a learning environment that was both sociologically and historically irrelevant and
oftentimes boring. I glanced at their frightened teacher, who
wore a look of pure amazement on her face at how curious and
articulate her students could be.

I finished the discussion by passing out my business card—
something that all the boys wanted—and told them if they wrote
(not called) me, I would send them a book about black people.
They agreed to do so, and after thanking them and telling them

to stay strong, I ended my discussion. They clapped, cheered, and asked me when I would be back again. I told them as soon as their teacher invited me.

As the teacher and I walked out of the classroom and back toward her office, she marveled at what had just occurred. She said that she "could never do that," and I agreed with her. She told me that she simply could not get their attention in the manner I had used, and I again agreed with her. She stopped outside of her office, looked me dead in the eye, and told me that perhaps she needed to stop teaching in the inner city because what she had learned in graduate school seemed totally irrelevant to her students. I agreed with her and told her that if she were unwilling to submit to a complete overhaul of what was necessary to teach black boys, she should quit and teach white children. She was not offended by this suggestion and actually seemed relieved that I was relating to her so frankly about black boys. I left her, and during the next three months sent eight books to the boys in her class.

I walked into the class that day with no idea as to what I was going to tell those boys. I knew that my message would be about how they should be warriors, but I didn't know how I was going to get there. Though it is an unpopular idea among educators to include spirituality in teaching, I think it is important to understand the African ancestral spirit that follows those who teach young blacks. On that particular day, I believe that the ancestors provided me with a relevant example that would capture the attention of the boys. I needed their attention, and the use of an illustration that was culturally relevant to them was important.

Raising boys to be African warriors requires a dedication beyond what most educators are willing to give and beyond what many parents are capable of, since it goes far beyond what

many of them *want* to do. It takes searching for a history that
has been lost, and then setting up venues where this history can
be taught. Because traditional educational settings are resistant
to helping children who have been designated as "special," "disruptive," and "incorrigible," Saturday mornings may have to be
sacrificed to do this. Likewise, parents and guardians of black
boys will have to begin an avid reading program with their sons
and learn about youth culture—something that parents may not
wish to do. As an educator, I believe that most, but not all, parents want their children to learn. But many are unwilling to provide supplemental black education and rely solely on schools to
teach their children. Educating Young Warriors entails going far
beyond traditional methods of teaching. Uri Treisman's research
at Berkeley did wonders in teaching young black children cal-
culus and other mathematics long after schools had given up
on them. Teachers such as Marva Collins who defied systems
and who had a vision for their students, unaffected by what was
said about them, have characterized the history of successful
educational strategies for black children. In the early 1970s, she
fought tooth and nail before she decided to break away from the
Chicago public school system to establish Westside Preparatory
in 1975. I have taught graduates of Westside Prep; they are
some of the most brilliant black students I've met, and several of
them have earned advanced degrees in a host of fields.

Educators, both black and white, are usually punished for
providing pedagogical innovations outside of what is required
by the school district. Indeed, the history of educating African
American children about who they are is a history of struggle.
Teaching Africans in America to read was illegal in most southern states and could result in death during the period of enslavement. Laurence Clifton Jones's 1909 establishment of Piney

Woods Country Life School outside of Jackson, Mississippi, was done with great risk to his life and to the lives of his students.

Carter G. Woodson's scathing indictment on how American Africans are *miseducated* reads like yesterday's newspaper. Woodson focuses nearly his entire critique on the issue of *control* of what black children learn. The twentieth century is peppered with accounts of the resistance to educating black children, including the integration of public schools following *Brown v. Board of Education.* It continues with the resistance encountered by those who advocate African-centered education for black children, particularly black boys.

In 1991, lawsuits were filed against Malcolm X Academy in Detroit for being an all-boys school and teaching an African-centered curriculum, despite the fact that the grades and standardized test scores were significantly higher than those of comparable boys in mixed classes. The Baseline Essays introduced into the Portland, Oregon, public school system in the 1980s were roundly criticized for their content. The fact that attendance and test scores were significantly higher than those of black children in traditional classes was ignored, yet no alternative curriculum was offered by "anti-Afrocentrists" decrying the "unscientific" nature of the essays. Dinesh D'Souza, like so many others critical of African-centered educational methods, seems more concerned with hegemonic control over curricula than innovative methods for teaching black children. This is particularly true of the young black male, the icon of poor educational achievement.

At the higher-education level, African-centered education has met resistance primarily by conservative white educators such as Arthur Schlesinger and Mary Lefkowitz. Lefkowitz's book *Not Out of Africa: How Afrocentrism Became an Excuse*

to Teach Myth as History was a full-frontal attack on the teachings of such educators as John Henrik Clarke, Molefi Asante,
and Marimba Ani. Lefkowitz's disingenuous attempt to portray
Afrocentricity as an educational plague visited upon innocent
black children is not so much an attack on the theory as it
is a defense against what she sees as a denigration of Western literature, history, and science. Arthur Schlesinger sees, in
near-apocalyptic terms, Afrocentricity as a direct attack against
Western knowledge, particularly as it relates to what black children need to know. Black academics, too, have contributed
their voices to criticizing African-centered approaches to higher
education. Henry Louis "Skip" Gates, chair of Harvard's Black
Studies Department, has been referred to by the *Chronicle of
Higher Education* as the "Booker T. Washington of Black Studies," a not-so-subtle reference to his ability to define the field of
Black Studies the way Washington defined education for black
people over a century ago. Gates's influence is viewed by serious African-centered scholars as unduly conservative and, in
many cases, misleading as to the importance of African-centered
worldviews. The firestorm that arose after his 1999 PBS special,
Wonders of the African World, centered on its condescending
portrayal of Africa and its people. Pejoratively referred to as
"Skip's World" and "Blunderer in the African World" by some,
the PBS travelogue was thoroughly criticized by African scholars who saw it as total distortion of Africa and its people. The
recent publication of Gates and Anthony Appiah's *Africana: The
Encyclopedia of the African and African-American Experience*,
portrayed by them as a "fulfillment" of W. E. B. Du Bois's dream
of an "Encyclopaedia Africana," is far from being such, and has
also been met with criticism. Many inaccuracies plagued the

first edition, which, ironically, did not even contain an entry for the word *Africa*!

It seems hypocritical that as long as black children receive overdoses of white culture in nearly all of their subjects, no attention was paid on how such knowledge generally failed to raise test scores or appreciably diminish school absenteeism. Yet when black educators achieve these two modest but necessary behaviors for learning, they are criticized for creating "myths" about human history and science. Forget that George Washington never took an ax to a cherry tree, threw a dollar over the Delaware, or stood up in a rowboat to get across that same river. Forget about the racism that pervaded American presidents from Washington through Eisenhower, as documented by Kenneth O'Reilly in *Nixon's Piano*. As Maulana Karenga has noted, much of Western history is self-congratulatory and full of myths that reinforce the notion of white superiority and black inferiority. Teaching black boys to understand their own history and its relationship to white supremacist history is an essential characteristic of educating them.

The Four Cs

The Ten Commitments are essential characteristics needed by those raising and teaching black boys. They should be the impetus for achieving four goals in the healthy development of young black men. These "Four Cs"—consciousness, commitment, cooperation, and community—summarize what I have learned from more than a quarter of a century of teaching and discovering what really works when educating black youth.

Consciousness

Black consciousness is being aware of who you are as an African in the *Maafa na Maangamizi*, realizing how you came to be in your present condition, and using that knowledge to understand your future. It is imbibing African culture at numerous levels in one's life and reflecting it in work and play.

I begin all of my classes at Morgan State University by asking my students, "Who are you?" The most common reply is that they are male, female, a freshman, a sophomore, an Alpha Kappa Alpha, or something else. It is rare that within the first two or three responses the students describe themselves as "African" or an "African in America." One may say that the absence of such descriptors merely proves how far removed the average black person is from their "African roots." I would agree with that and add simply that it is precisely this distance from their African selves that prevents them from learning effectively. Psychologist Na'im Akbar says that four disordered personalities arise from American Africans who imbibe heavily of European culture at the expense of connecting with their African selves:

Alien-Self Disorders—"These are the growing number of American Africans in recent years who have been socialized in families with primarily materialistic goals. They see themselves as material and evaluate their worth by the prevalence of material accouterments which they possess. . . ." Akbar says that the alien-self disorder is increasingly prevalent among professional American Africans who seek to imitate the dominant culture of the United States. Known as "Afro-Saxons" among many, sociologist Nathan Hare calls them the "black Anglo-Saxons" because of their absorption of white middle-class culture and its accompanying disorders.

Anti-Self Disorders—This disorder is characterized by a near-complete identification with the dominant American culture. They exhibit hostility toward other American Africans, and may work actively against them if they are in a position of authority within white America. Viewed by whites as a "good Negro," these American Africans are Super Slaves to a culture that rewards them for opposing their African American cultural roots. They are the exact opposite of Norman Mailer's idea of the "White Negro" and seek approval from whites, which may even be manifested in marrying members of the group.

Self-Destructive Disorders—Oppression creates environments where individuals destroy themselves. These conditions can lead to homicidal violence; those on the outside may see drug dealing, prostitution, and pimping as "natural" for the group. Lacking consciousness of self leads to self-destructive behavior in a culture that encourages deracinated people. American Africans who fit this description are not necessarily poor and unemployed; indeed, they can be wealthy and famous but prone to behavior that demonstrates low self-esteem and the tendency toward taking risks. Their identity is viewed as antithetical to "mainstream" Eurocentric values, and they are usually feared by the dominant society because of their antisocial behavior.

Organic Disorders—Pollution, lead-based paint, and other environmental factors can lead to disorders that stunt the healthy growth of black boys. According to the National Insti-

tute of Allergy and Infectious Diseases, American Africans were
three to four times more likely than whites to be hospitalized
for asthma, and were four to six times more likely to die from it.
"Poverty, substandard housing that results in increased exposure
to certain indoor allergens, lack of education, inadequate access
to health care, and the failure to take appropriate medications
may all contribute to the risk of having a severe asthma attack or,
more tragically, of dying from asthma." Man-made substances
such as lead, asbestos, and airborne carcinogens can breed mental disabilities, asthma, and higher rates of cancer in African
American children and can subsidize the psychological damage
done to many black boys at young ages.

These disorders arise naturally from an environment that
does not reinforce the healthy development of black identity
in young American African boys. Implicit in white curricula
are books, films, and other learning materials that buttress the
notion that being white is something positive and contributes to
the general well-being of the planet. This "white consciousness"
is not even objectified, so it makes it nearly impossible to have
a discussion about it. "Being white" means being "American," a
good citizen, and a human being, while "being black" implies the
Du Boisian notion of "twoness" and alienation. In *Souls of Black
Folk,* Du Bois said: "One ever feels his twoness—an American, a
Negro; two souls, two thoughts, two unreconciled strivings; two
warring ideals in one dark body, whose dogged strength alone
keeps it from being torn asunder."

I believe that Du Bois's "twoness" does reside in many, but not
all, American Africans. Raising a black child does not necessarily
mean that he or she will be confused about his or her racial identity. This phrase from Du Bois is often quoted to indicate that at

best American Africans will grow up confused about who they are. An early commitment to raising black consciousness and secure American African children will guarantee that they will grow up without a divided racial identity.

Consciousness is the first and most fundamental step in raising healthy black boys in America. A consciousness of how one "fits" into the *Maafa na Maangamizi* and a world reeling from racism allows young black boys to see themselves in a far broader context than what is taught to them in schools. For educators to reconnect the links between young Africans in America and their ancestors is important. The beginning of this can take the form of reading stories of ancient Africa aloud to preschool black boys. Finding suitable books is much easier than it was even ten years ago; the availability of African-centered materials has grown considerably. Here are some steps that can be taken to build a consciousness of the African self among American African boys:

Begin at young ages to read aloud to boys about American African heroes and sheroes. The late child psychologist Bruno Bettelheim said that the four most beautiful words in a child's ear are "Once upon a time." I agree, and these words can introduce black boys to the fascinating history of Africans in the *Maafa na Maangamizi.* Reading aloud to black boys creates an early love of imagination and understanding of the world they live in and their place within it.

Insist that school systems recognize various cultural holidays in schools that are relevant to Africans in the Maafa na Maangamizi. The most celebrated holiday devoted to American African history is Martin Luther King Jr.'s birthday. In many areas, its celebration remains controversial, with some school systems grumbling about its "intrusion" on the academic calendar. Black History Month follows close behind, with some schools mounting sophisticated programs that celebrate the history of black people.

This is as it should be, and parents can suggest to schools other notable days such as Malcolm X's birthday on May 19, pre-Kwanzaa celebrations, and other events that detail the history of American Africans. School calendars in general should celebrate a variety of ethnic holidays pertaining to all persons. I am amused when I see nearly all-black elementary schools asking their students to wear green on St. Patrick's Day when virtually none of the students have any ancestral connection to Ireland. These same schools will ignore other holidays and events that are more salient to black children, such as Kwanzaa, deeming them "too ethnic."

Provide a broad listening repertoire to black boys that includes jazz, reggae, rhythm and blues, gospel, funk, symphonic works by black composers, rap, and soul. Chuck Jackson, a 1960s R & B singer, once told me that music in the black community "turns over" about once every eight years. Rap has been around for over twenty. Young people today admittedly say that they listen to rap more than R & B. Jazz and blues artists are often relegated to being "old school" and "too adult." Black parents, educators, and children should encourage *one another* to understand and appreciate the variety of music produced by black artists. Parents can encourage "listening nights" instead of "viewing nights" during which they share one another's favorite music.

Take opportunities to visit museums, library exhibits, and other community activities that present black history. When necessary, connect with Warrior Method parents to mount political influence that will force systems to provide such attractions. Art museums, libraries, and other cultural centers have large discretion over which exhibits they will mount and how long they will be displayed. Parents and teachers of black students should influence such decisions through performing volunteer activities and suggesting ideas for exhibits and displays. The National Museum of African American History and Culture is the most visited museum in Washington, DC, and provides an emotional and informative journey for children and adults alike.

Encourage black houses of worship to supplement your boys' education by having at least three hours of classes per week devoted to the study of black history. Most American African faith communities celebrate the same holidays that schools do. They should go beyond that by offering Saturday morning classes that teach black history to young people. At an automobile plant not far from Fisk University, workers relocating from Japan opened Saturday schools for their children to ensure their continued understanding of Japanese culture while in Tennessee. Churches can be instrumental in teaching children black world history by offering similar courses.

On more than one occasion I have had the privilege of speaking in black churches during February, surrounded by white angels, Jesuses, and prophets. I point out to my audience the need to substitute these powerful images with black angels and religious figures in order to create a more balanced view of religion. Black faith communities can be extremely influential institutions in shaping the consciousness of black boys even before they go to school.

Provide educational films that teach the history of Africa, the period of enslavement, and its aftermath. The horrors of enslavement and the fate of its victims should be taught to black boys in a manner similar to what is taught to young Jewish children about the Holocaust. I know black parents who avoid exposing their sons to the horrors of enslavement, lynching, apartheid, and violence toward American Africans. This expensive proposition will be paid for by their development of a naive view of world history. Teaching this history should be done carefully, but it should be done. Black children who have an understanding of the "stony road" trod by their ancestors are better prepared to understand current challenges facing black communities around the world.

Expand images of Africa beyond those of famine, war, and disaster that characterize coverage of the continent by news organizations. Travelogues that include elephants, giraffes, and hyenas are good, but they limit the view of Africa as the proverbial "dark continent." Black children need to understand their connection to the continent by being exposed to its folklore, culture, customs, clothing, and people. They need to know their roots in West Africa so that they are rooted in their history. I am amused when I see European Americans who encourage their children to understand their Italian, French, German, or English roots yet belittle educators who do the same with black children's connection to Africa. Such attitudes develop the deeply held notion that Africa contributed virtually nothing to world history or culture. Fallacies such as these need to be corrected so that a healthy view of Africa can be instilled in the minds of black *and* white children.

I recently subscribed to a service from my cellular phone provider that automatically sends customized news about Africa directly to my phone. All of the short headlines were about war, famine, disease, and death. No human-interest stories. Nothing good. No uplifting stories about a continent whose beauty, people, and culture are some of the most diverse in the world. Those who glean the wire services looking for some good news about Africa would think that it is indeed the "dark continent" that has been imprinted on the minds of the world for the past five hundred years.

Encourage the wearing of African clothing at young ages. All parents complain about how their children dress. It is a part of growing up. The popularity of *Kente* cloth and other African fabrics makes it easier for parents to teach their sons about African clothing and its meanings. While dress is no indicator of cultural commitment, it can be an easy way to teach lessons about one's heritage. Green ties on St. Patrick's Day; red, white, and blue on the Fourth of July; and clothing decorated with Confederate flags are cultural statements about one's heritage. Clothing is an easy way to teach people about their history, and this includes black boys as well.

At a Black History Month speaking engagement I spoke to an attractive black family who had agreed that on Fridays they would all wear African clothing to work or school. The parents as well as their two teenage sons saw the clothing as both a statement and a way of teaching the importance of connections to Africa. The father told me how they knew the meaning of the clothing, where it was from, and under which circumstances it was worn. Too often generalizations are made about the continent of Africa, rather than citing information pertaining to individual African nations. Ghanaian clothing, for example, differs from South African clothing, and both differ from that which is worn in East Africa.

The need for "raising black consciousness" among black children is not new and will remain as long as racism surrounds them. Consciousness building is a lifelong process that begins in early childhood. It is a subtle process that can occur under a variety of circumstances. Sitting at the dinner table, wandering through the grocery store, paying a bill, or watching television with black boys—all can be the backdrop for lessons on who they are, where they have been, and where they are going. As I write this, the film *Black Panther* not only broke box office records, but was viewed by black families celebrating their connections to Africa. Educating black children can take place in venues outside of the classroom as well as inside.

Finally, black boys should also be encouraged to talk about their feelings, both good and bad. This is particularly critical when it comes to their feelings about girls and women.

While more will be said about this later, young black boys must understand the importance of seeing females as part of the sacred male-female bond so common in precolonial Africa and so absent today. Writer and critic Ayi Kwei Armah talks about the beauty of the relationship between black men and women and argues in *Two Thousand Seasons* that the destroyers (white supremacists) were and are always attempting to disrupt the healthy development of black men and women with each other.

"There is no beauty but in relationships. Nothing cut off by itself is beautiful. Never can things in destructive relationships be beautiful.

"All beauty is in the creative purpose of our relationships. All ugliness is in the destructive aims of the destroyer's arrangements."

Commitment

The effort of raising consciousness in black boys and in oneself will inevitably lead to a commitment to them. The idea that black boys are a "throwaway generation" and are expendable is often an unconscious reality in schools and institutions that deal with them. I once asked a workshop composed primarily of white elementary school teachers to write on slips of paper something they *did not* like to do as teachers, but not to include their names. When I read them aloud to the group, I saw on one, "I do not like to touch my black boys." I had to withhold my anger in front of the group as I read the statement, and I thought how unfortunate the black boys were in the class of this "teacher" who did not like to tie their unlaced shoe, or comfort them if they scraped their knee in a playground fall. Such feelings of loathing indicate the success of dehumanizing young black males even among elementary school teachers.

It is important to understand how criminalizing black males in America has a long and sordid history and reinforces negative stereotypes about them. Charshee McIntyre said that studying the imprisonment patterns of black males is a strong indicator of how representing black males as dangerous became a self-fulfilling prophecy. For example, although Africans in Pennsylvania made up only 2.4 percent of the population in 1800, the decennial censuses in Chart 1 indicate their population in the Walnut Street Jail, known historically as "the cradle of modern penitentiaries."

CHART 1: PERCENTAGE OF BLACK MALES IN WALNUT STREET JAIL, 1790–1830

Year	% African American Males
1790	4.6%
1800	8.5%
1810	9.4%
1820	8.8%
1830	8.3%

Source: *Criminalizing a Race: Free Blacks During Slavery*, Charshee Lawrence-McIntyre. New York: Kayode Publications, 1992, pp. 166, 167.

Essentially, black males were "overrepresented" in the prison system two hundred years ago, the same way they are overrepresented today. More recently, Michelle Alexander in her book, *The New Jim Crow: Mass Incarceration in the Age of Color-blindness,* has described this "overrepresentation" as historical, deliberate, and increasing. There is roughly a 4:1 historical ratio of black males in the general population to those in prison. This is a remarkably consistent pattern that has held steadily since such records have been kept. McIntyre and Alexander both note how anyone who is committed to understanding contemporary black males must connect the dots between such esoteric data and the systems in place that create such patterns of incarceration. I agree. It is not a waste of time for the committed educator, parent, or social worker to read *what happened* to black men in this country in order to understand *what is happening* to black boys today.

A case in point: I got a call from a mother whose eleven-year-old son was expelled from school for "stealing $37.00 out of his teacher's purse." She had exhausted all of her appeals to get the suspension expunged from Todd's fifth-grade record. Todd was depressed when I saw him. An honor student with no blemishes on his record and no discipline problems, he simply happened to be the last student in the class on the day when his teacher's purse had been rifled. Added to the "incriminating" evidence was the fact that he had $50 on him at the time he was confronted about the missing money. Even though his mother had given him the $50 to pay a bill after school that day, her alibi was ignored, and a police officer dutifully took a "victim's report" from the white woman who reported the theft. Todd made perfect fodder for a system that is set on criminalizing black boys at the youngest age possible.

I had seen too many incidents like this before, and knew that many others had escaped my attention. There is one common element in how such scenarios are brought to the attention of therapists and attorneys, and that is if the child has a Warrior Method parent, teacher, or guardian. Todd's mother fit the description of such a parent. Single, poor, and living in public housing, she was obsessively involved with the education of her two sons. She called my office for an appointment. When she arrived, she had the necessary documents in the case and explained that she needed an advocate for her son so that this incident would not be on his record. Organized and angry, she told me that she believed that her son was innocent and that the teacher felt threatened by his assertive and intelligent behavior, particularly when it came to discussing racial issues in his social studies class.

They came to me on the first day of his suspension, and I was impressed with the confidence exhibited by both Todd and his mother. He didn't strike me as a thief; based solely on the evidence that they presented, I called the teacher, principal, and "downtown" for appointments to have his case reopened.

I have learned that systems, particularly educational systems, are often remarkably sloppy when they go after young black males. It is as if those who mistreat black boys feel sanctioned to do nearly anything to them with impunity. Todd was no exception. Poor record keeping, a weak black principal who was thankful for having a job at a predominantly white school, and a tired bureaucrat at administrative headquarters who simply wanted Todd, his mother, and me to go away were quick to have the charges expunged. The teacher wanted both her money and a criminal, and Todd happened to be handy. One week after the apology and a sanitized record, a *white* boy "turned himself in" after his mother discovered an amount of money larger than his allowance in his bedroom. *He* had been the last one in the teacher's classroom, not Todd, but somehow he received only a *reprimand* because he was "honest" in returning the money. It is impossible not to see a double standard at work in this case and in most cases involving how black and white boys are treated by educational and legal systems.

The second of the Four Cs—commitment—is achieved simply by doing the "right thing" with regard to black boys. Black boys are often without advocates in a nation frequently bent on demoralizing and destroying them physically, spiritually, and emotionally. For every Todd who is proven innocent, there are many other black boys who are falsely accused by persons who simply want them out of the way or because they fit a certain description. Commitment is putting the first C—consciousness—into action, and being unrelenting in the pursuit of justice for black boys. It emphasizes the heart rather than the head; knowledge of your son's character arises from the familiarity gained after being conscious of your son and the systems through which he must travel. There is only one indication of commitment to black boys: the willingness to intervene on their behalf at any level to enhance their life chances.

Cooperation

Cooperation in raising black boys takes place at several levels. Ideally it should involve several members of the immediate family—something that is diminishing as single parenting and divorce rates increase within American African communities. Cooperation includes understanding the historical relationship that school systems played in educating black children, and how relationships between black men and black women were damaged by enslavement and its impact on the black family. The closeness necessary between outside agencies—most notably schools—and those raising black children is not understood as well as it should be. Those committed to raising Cinque's sons require a thorough understanding of how cooperative relationships both outside *and* inside black families are under assault by American institutions.

Cooperation and Black Schools. The African proverb "It takes a village to raise a child" is part of the national lexicon on how to raise at-risk children. From White Houses to the street, the proverb is quoted to acknowledge how systems *and* parents are responsible for rearing children in America. Educator Jawanza Kunjufu cynically says that the proverb presupposes that there is a *functional* village to raise the child, a detail that is all too often lacking.

The destruction of the "village" took place over the past century as black families migrated north during the 1920s and 1930s and reinvented various institutions to accommodate their sense of community. The "storefront church" on the south side was the reincarnation of the one-room church in rural Mississippi. The country juke joint became the local honky-tonk as African Americans refined the blues and jazz born in the cotton fields of the Deep South. Most regrettable during this transition was the inability to duplicate educational systems that had been heavily influenced by the presence of black colleges and universities such as Hampton, Fisk, and Tougaloo. "Urban education" became synonymous with black education and was associated with unresponsive administrations, inefficiency, and lack of materials.

The segregation patterns of the South persisted in the North, however, and the ironic benefits of the entire *Plessy v. Ferguson* era were that segregated systems actually allowed for a more intact presentation of black culture and history to students. The Lake Mohonk Conferences, June 4–6, 1890, and June 3–5, 1891, give a clear understanding of the role of racism in the education of black people. Held in upstate New York, they occurred shortly after the period of enslavement to discuss the "Negro Question." Rutherford B. Hayes, credited with the "Compromise of 1877," which effectively disenfranchised southern blacks of nearly all of the gains of Reconstruction, convened the conferences and called for an emphasis on industrial education to "uplift the Negro." What was important about these conferences is that they saw American Africans as newly freed beasts of burden in need of guidance in how to be "good citizens." Part of the historic Du Bois/Washington debate was Du Bois's disagreement with the emphasis on industrial education at the expense of the liberal arts. Du Bois and Woodson both saw education as liberation and challenged the educational philosophy of Mohonk that relegated American Africans to the subservience of a strictly labor class.

"Lift Every Voice and Sing," part of the music repertoire of most black children prior to *Brown,* was slowly phased out after the decision. Likewise, black principals and other "role models" were forced into early retirement due to the "merger" of black and white schools during the 1960s and 1970s. In the South alone, some fifteen hundred black administrators lost their jobs directly because of these mergers, a fact often overlooked by integration advocates.

This should not be construed as a rationale for maintaining racially segregated school systems, but as an honest acknowledgment that *Brown v. Board* in 1954 forced American African educators and parents to relinquish to faceless bureaucracies what control they did have over their children's education. Attempts to gain control over the damaging effects of the desegregation order took the form of demonstrations in the infamous 1968 Ocean Hill–Brownsville controversy in Brooklyn, New York. Warrior Method parents tried unsuccessfully to regain local control over curriculum development from a centralized bureaucracy that ignored the needs of the nearly all-black school district.

The cry for all-black schools, and, specifically, all-black male schools, should be viewed as a historical correction over the problems associated with *Brown v. Board.* The "separate but equal" system that had existed for sixty years in the United States was "remedied" by moving bodies (black and white children) rather than bureaucracies. White schools were deemed superior to black schools and therefore "integrating" them with black children would assure higher learning and school performance. White schools with black children were thought to be the most efficient way of eliminating patterns of discrimination.

Predictably, the busing riots of the 1970s showed once again how deeply resistant many whites were to racially integrated education and exposed their underlying fears of miscegenation. What needed to be bused from white to black school districts were tax dollars that were unfairly distributed in ways that ensured the "inferiority" of black schools. *Time* magazine in a cover story timidly asked a few years ago if integration had "failed." The answer is yes, in that it did not address the educational needs of American African children. Neither did it usher in the "Beloved Community" King called for in his historic "I Have a Dream" speech.

Cooperation Between Black Men and Women. Undoubtedly the greatest impact that racism had on Africans in the *Maafa na Maangamizi* was the destruction of the African family, especially the relationship between men and women. The principle of "twinness" reflected in the literature and art of West African culture, where American African ancestral ties lie, shows the sacredness of the relationship between men and women. On my visits to Ghana, I never fail to spend time watching men and women make *foo-foo*, a dumplinglike mixture of flour, oil, and yeast. The man plunges a six-foot pestle from above his head into the rounded bowl while the woman gracefully reshapes the dough with her nimble fingers. The rhythm of the process is hypnotic and illustrates the connection that must exist between a man and woman when making the bread. One seventy-five-year-old woman told me that never once had she seen a man or woman hurt while making the dumpling, though toes and fingers are at stake as the delicacy takes shape.

Similar balances exist among Ghanaian men and women who do a brisk trade in *Kente* cloth, a popular fabric among American Africans and symbolic of the ties between blacks in the United States and West Africa. Though viewed as "sexist" because only men are allowed to weave it, I have spoken to Ghanaian women and men who say that this division of labor is protective of the woman; the lower body is used in the making of the cloth and can strain the reproductive organs of women and lead to miscarriage if they are pregnant. The social balance is evidenced by the fact that women handle *all* the business associated with the cloth's packaging, distribution, and sales.

Black men and women in America can restore the historical balance between them by surrounding their sons with cultural artifacts and celebrations that reinforce a positive view of West Africa. They can encourage cooperative child rearing among themselves regardless of their marital status.

The "absent black father," though exaggerated in many instances by the media, can continue an active role in his son's life, particularly as it relates to his education. Again, it is important to mention that understanding how racism works to mutate relationships among blacks is critical in raising and educating healthy black boys in America.

Black boys will benefit from understanding the cooperative relationship between black men and women in the struggle against racism and the restoration of African values. There will be a diminished emphasis on material possessions such as "designer clothing" and athletic shoes that commodify black boys into becoming, as George Curry puts it, "advertising billboards for the clothing industry."

Cooperation should also focus on sharing parenting duties with single parents. In 2014, single women headed 29 percent of African American households, outnumbering married couples living together (26 percent) by 3 percent. Fifteen percent of households are headed by single black men, thus making 44 percent of black families single-parent households. Since the 1980s, there has been a trend that more American African children are residing in homes with single parents than married couples. The same goes for white families. Twenty-six percent of white families are single-parent households, up from 19 percent in the 1980s.

It is also important to understand that parenting must be redefined to include a *functional* "village" for young black males. This village is the extended family that nurtured the black family during enslavement and beyond. Herbert Gutman has shown that, despite rumors to the contrary, the African American family remained remarkably intact during the years following enslavement. He argues that the idea of the "disorganized black family" exaggerated by Patrick Moynihan in 1965 was more myth than reality. What has occurred since the Vietnam War is an increase in single parenting, which coincides with the increased criminalization of American African males and their subsequent incarceration.

This unbalanced black sex ratio (defined as the number of men per one hundred women) is at an all-time low (83:100) and does not include men who are gay, confirmed bachelors, with white women, or incarcerated.

These numbers should not be construed to mean that women must have a man in order to be complete. It simply points out the lack of choices that American African women have if they desire heterosexual marriage and a traditional nuclear family. Black boys shoulder a disproportionate amount of the frustration since more single women are parenting without adult males to serve as role models. Much has been written and discussed about how young black males may become the inadvertent victims of the frustration that their mothers feel toward the absent fathers. In one scene from John Singleton's

Boyz in the Hood, a single mother turns to her pubescent son and says, rather matter-of-factly, "Your daddy ain't shit, your brother ain't shit, and you ain't gonna be shit." The son is clearly frustrated and angry at the words. Although the movie was fictional, I have witnessed many such scenes both in public and in private.

The need to incorporate many people, particularly black men, in the rearing of black boys should be done in both informal and formal ways. Informally, American African families have always solicited the help of relatives and friends for babysitting, entertainment, and household chores. What has been missing are more formal ways that take advantage of our community institutions. Following are some ways we can rebuild the infrastructure of the "village" Kunjufu speaks of:

Establish more "Mother's Day/Evening Out" programs at American African churches so that single parents can get relief from parenting. Many black houses of worship in the American African community already provide free day/night care on particular days so that mothers and fathers can leave their young children and enjoy a day alone or a night out on the town with their friends. This encourages a strong connection between houses of worship and single black parents and gives black elders a chance to mentor young children.

Make volunteering with black boys for five hours a month an initiation rite for all members of black social organizations. While most black organizations have volunteer service incorporated into their charters, they should require that new initiates work with black boys for five hours per month for a stipulated period. This will foster an attitude within the new member that working with young black boys is a priority and an obligation. It will also aid in establishing emotional ties with the new members, which will hopefully extend beyond the initiation period.

Encourage adoption among black houses of worship. The One Church, One Child Program, which began in 1980 under George Clements, a Catholic priest, now boasts over twenty-two hundred black churches in thirty-five states that have adopted more than ten thousand youngsters in their churches. The program recruits families within its membership who wish to adopt black children, then works with adoption agencies for placement. This program is a model for what needs to be a nationwide effort to place black boys who are traditionally the least likely to be adopted into stable homes.

Create reading groups sponsored by black male civic and religious groups that support black boys reading about American African culture and life. If civic and religious groups can sponsor sports teams for black boys, they can expand their programs to include reading clubs as well. A good venue for such places is the increasing number of black-owned bookstores. Establishing a regular reading club makes good business sense for the owner and provides a perfect atmosphere for black boys. Libraries, too, are good locations for such clubs; once again, creating reading groups is a low-cost investment for black churches wishing to increase reading skills among their young members.

Because of the dwindling number of two-parent households, cooperative child rearing has become a central concern in the black family. Although national organizations such as 100 Black Men, black fraternities, and other groups are becoming more active in the cooperative rearing of black boys, more can be done. This goal should be high on the agenda of any black organization that claims as its purpose the alleviation of problems within American African communities.

Community

At the end of the day, community may be the most important of all the Four Cs since it advocates Black and Gray Way parents challenging the systems that too often hurt, maim, and destroy self-esteem and, thus, the healthy development of black boys. Warrior Method parents understand the necessity of creating alternative systems to provide for the healthy development of their sons.

American Africans are fond of comparing their conflicts with one another to "crabs in a barrel." We focus on how the crabs are fighting each other and particularly how they "pull each other down" when a successful one begins its long and difficult climb to the "top of the barrel."

We rarely ask how these metaphorical crabs got in "the barrel" in the first place, and even more importantly, what does "the barrel" represent?

It is as if the device that imprisons the creatures is forgotten in our metaphor of the warring and jealous crabs. Perhaps it is because it is easier to discuss victims rather than perpetrators, and individuals rather than systems.

Understanding "the barrel" is the most important analysis that American Africans can engage in, eclipsed only by how we get out of and then destroy "the barrel" in which we are imprisoned.

Political and social pressure on systems through which black boys pass should be monitored on several levels to ensure that no black boy becomes a victim of racism. It is amazing how little contemporary American Africans know about the history of education in their communities. The popular media exalts the histories of Booker T. Washington and George Washington Carver, as they should, but neglect to discuss the works of Carter G. Woodson, John Henrik Clarke, and Mary Church Terrell, who taught the importance of Warrior Method activism. What is even more astonishing is how current educators, both black and nonblack, lack understanding of how local, state, and federal governments actively sought, in deliberate and systematic ways, the disenfranchisement of black education.

Warrior Method parents and teachers must strive to teach those around them about American African educational history so that what seems to be "radical" is viewed in the context of the historical struggle to provide quality education for black children. The confrontations in Little Rock, Ocean Hill, Brownsville, the University of Mississippi, Piney Woods, and the University of Alabama and the establishment of historically black colleges and universities (HBCUs) are in the best tradition of pushing toward educational opportunities for black children. The civil rights movement itself was fueled primarily by struggles to dismantle white supremacy in school systems that had legally excluded blacks since *Plessy*. The violence that resulted from integrating the Universities of Mississippi and Alabama is part of a long tradition of white resistance to the education of black children; it continues today with discussions of vouchers and charter schools. Warrior Method parents understand that only in rare instances have white school systems been seriously committed to educating black children. This is a difficult idea to accept, especially by White Way parents, but the proof exists in the historical record.

But more needs to be done. Medical care, decent housing, political empowerment, and affordable day care should be
moved to the top of the agendas of those who want the best for
black boys. Several specific strategies can be taught and adopted
by black institutions to ensure that this occurs:

*Monitoring and attending school board meetings in school dis-
tricts.* The importance of black parents being politically involved
with local school boards cannot be overemphasized. Often only
crises, such as the closing of a cherished school, bring black
parents to school board meetings, and the overall flow of school
board decisions is lost. Churches and other black civic organizations should send to school board meetings designated monitors,
who then disseminate board decisions to their constituents. The
names and addresses of each board member should be printed
in newsletters and bulletins, so that between meetings parents
can lobby on critical issues that affect their children.

*Using Title VI of the 1964 Civil Rights Act to ensure the equi-
table distribution of federal dollars for local projects.* Henri
Brooks, former chair of the Tennessee State Black Caucus,
says that Title VI of the 1964 U.S. Civil Rights Act is the most
neglected part of the 1960s civil rights legislation. Title VI specifically calls for the equitable, nondiscriminatory distribution of
federal funds to local governments. Under this act, municipali-
ties are obligated to ensure that all segments of the community
are represented on the boards responsible for the distribution
of funds to local businesses, arts organizations, social programs,
etc. Organizations serving the needs of black people have overlooked their right to sue under this legislation. Tracing how
federal funds were used at the state and local levels could pro-

vide the basis for a class-action lawsuit that could result in more dollars for programs targeting black youth.

Creating political action committees (PACs) that serve the special interests of the black community. Political action in black communities has a long and rich history that should continue by increasing the number of PACs for targeted purposes. PACs have become a political reality in the United States and blacks can use them to influence the outcome of elections and legislation that affect their lives. Black elected officials should place a high priority on the formation of PACs, and these officials should educate their constituents about their need.

Both the 2008 and 2012 national elections showed the importance of black persons engaging cooperatively in national elections. News organizations only recently began focusing on the disenfranchisement of black people during the 2016 presidential election, yet it was the biggest story of the political year. The denial of access to voting targeting black and Latino voters, and voter suppression laws, is illustrative of the fragility of America when it comes to ensuring the rights of persons of color. Voter ID laws supposedly enacted to prevent the mythical idea of "voter fraud" are only the current manifestation of the historical determination to disenfranchise blacks from the most fundamental right America supposedly provides to all citizens—voting. No less than the provisions of the Fifteenth Amendment were at stake during the 2000 elections, yet Americans—white and black—thought that "accepting the results" was more important than ensuring the rights of disenfranchised voters. Young Warriors should be thoroughly versed regarding the events in the United States during November and December of 2000. They should understand how there is no end to the lengths to which white supremacists will go in order to limit the voices of blacks, even though it may mean scuttling the law and ignoring the Constitution. Some attribute the major congressional shift of 1996, particularly in the House of Representatives, to the large turnout of black voters. Similarly, more accountability from Democratic candidates should be demanded by black voters since an overwhelming number (90 percent) support the party. Black elected officials—overwhelmingly Democratic—need to get voters registered and educate their supporters. In addition, they must agitate for national Democratic leaders to devote more attention to the needs of black communities at all times.

Targeting for selective buying businesses that have a history of harassing and/or underemploying American Africans, particularly boys. The boycott remains a most effective way to achieve equity for American Africans. Nike, South Carolina, NBC, and other entities have yielded to requests for representation on boards and television shows, and have agreed to the removal of offensive symbols, all due to boycotts. Nothing effects quicker change than a focused effort by African Americans practicing selective buying of a company's product. Clothing companies whose markets are urban black males are particularly vulnerable to selective buying campaigns, and they should be made aware of the ramifications of their practices toward our youth and our collective power.

Systematically writing congressional representatives to make sure they are responsive to legislation that affects the lives of black children. One of the most effective yet neglected political-action strategies is as old as America: writing letters to lawmakers. The Internet and social media such as Facebook and Twitter make this even easier, and groups such as the National Black Child Development Institute (www.nbcdi.org) actually monitor at the national level legislation that will have impact on black youth.

Mailing lists of key political figures must contain the names and addresses of Warrior Method parents. The nonglamorous work of parsing the esoteric language of bills and legislative agendas is time-consuming and tedious, but it has to be done. I have participated in and encouraged others in letter-writing campaigns that were highly successful in blocking legislation that was egregious to young American African males.

Creating booster clubs that encourage the purchase of computer technology for black children. The recently discussed "digital gap" between whites and people of color is primarily economic. It is important that American African children become acquainted at young ages with what arguably will be the most important educational and cultural revolution in the first quarter of the twenty-first century. Gifts of computers or laptops instead of game machines are a good investment in our boys' future. Competitions sponsored by black civic organizations should have computers as first, second, and third prizes. Historically black colleges and universities, often located in depressed economic areas, can build educational bridges between their computer labs and the community. The goal of all these efforts is to keep American African children at a pace that will make them technologically competitive with other ethnic groups.

Organizing groups of American African houses of worship to build educational facilities to meet the needs of black children.

I recently spoke to a group of black ministers who asked what they could do as a group to help black boys in their community. I told them to place 50 percent of their fourth Sunday offering into an escrow account for one year and, with this initial capital, build a K–12 school. I then told them to continue the offering indefinitely to pay for the salaries of the teachers and administrators who would be employed in the school. The look of surprise on their faces was followed by many reasons why this was too great of a project. One minister said this was a "larger idea than what they had in mind" and that they thought the creation of a sports team or some other small project would be more feasible. I estimated that within the room there was conservatively $500,000 per week being placed in banks by the churches. I was essentially asking them for half of that during one offering to go for a school that would educate our children. There was resistance to this suggestion because of the symbolic role that black church buildings play in American African communities. They are often seen as monuments to a minister's business prowess and are rarely used more than two or three times per week.

This is not an indictment of misplaced priorities among black clergy but a call to rearrange existing priorities relative to educating black boys. Most black churches have some form of educational outreach ranging from day care to tutoring. In some cases churches run full-time accredited schools, paid for by members of the congregation. The advent of the "mega" black church—churches with more than three thousand members—should make building schools easier than in the past. Forming educational consortiums across denominations can bring smaller houses of worship into the educational process without burdening them financially.

Encouraging black houses of worship to create credit unions for the communities they serve. One of the principles of the American African holiday *Kwanzaa* is *Ujamaa* (pronounced UU-jah-mah), translated as "cooperative economics." Similar to the cooperative education of children that churches can establish, credit unions can be built that will help members regain a good credit rating, purchase homes, and establish small businesses. I know of several large urban churches who have done this without indulging in the dubious practice of creating "prosperity ministries," which often emphasize dollars over spiritual growth.

Placing money in American African–owned banks. While many communities do not have black-owned banks (as of this writing, there were thirty-eight black-owned banks and credit unions left in the United States), those that do should actively court black dollars of individuals, businesses, and churches. Individuals should also do as much business with these banks as possible so that community money can be reinvested in the community. This is a simple yet effective way of creating wealth for impoverished black communities, and it is similar to what other ethnic communities have done. Other options include using online black banking services that are sensitive to the needs of black consumers. Where black banks do not exist, community leaders should cultivate a close relationship between the institutions they represent and bank officers so that projects that are directly related to the surrounding community can be realized.

Sponsoring summer-abroad study programs in Africa. In my years as a college professor, I have been fortunate to see many of my students travel to Africa, a rewarding experience because it brings an abstract notion to life. I have witnessed firsthand the changes that take place in these students. They return energized and committed to teaching their peers more about the language, customs, and culture of Africa. I know black civic groups that sponsor winter tours to Europe for skiing vacations but avoid sending groups to Ghana, Senegal, or other West African nations. Most people—black and nonblack—after being fed *anti-African* ideas from the first day of their formal education, never consider Africa as a travel destination. Sponsoring tour groups with children and adults is an investment in their future; it gives them a much more realistic view of the ancestral home of American Africans.

Are these "big" agenda items? Yes. Are they feasible for all communities? No. Are there historical precedents for all of them? Yes. In the final analysis, community, the last of the Four Cs, encourages those interested in the well-being of black boys to become politically and socially involved in their lives. That's it.

The previous chapters outlined the necessary values, ideas, and knowledge to raise black boys. The following chapters, entitled the Seasons of Our Sons, will outline what our sons face as they grow from boys to men.

5

The Seasons of Our Sons: Spring, Conception to Four

> Ole Missus and young Missus told the little slave
> children that the stork brought the white babies to
> their mothers, but that the slave children were all
> hatched out from buzzards' eggs. And we believed it
> was true. —KATIE SUTTON, SLAVE[*]

Conception Through Four Years

The first rite of passage for humans is birth, and for black boys
the first year of life is one of the most dangerous on earth. The
outmoded term *third-world nation* is often used to describe
countries in the so-called "developing world." These developing
countries have high infant mortality rates. *The mortality rate
for American African children during their first year of life is
comparable to that of infants born in Libya.* As with other statistics, if the infant mortality rate for white babies were identical to that of black babies, there is no doubt in my mind that a
national crisis would be declared and millions of dollars would
be spent on pre- and postnatal care to ensure that white babies

---

[*] Recorded during the Federal Writers' Project of the 1930s and 1940s. Referenced in
James Mellon's *Bullwhip Days* (1988), Avon Books.

would survive their first year of life. The "good news" is that the infant mortality rate for American African infants both male and female decreased from 14.3 to 11.11 per 1,000 births from 2005 to 2013, a trend that hopefully will continue as more black families have access to pre- and postnatal health care. That the infant mortality rate of black children in the United States is nearly identical to those children born in Libya (11.1 per 1,000), Tonga (11.6 per 1,000), and Mexico (11.9 per 1,000) is evidence of why the first year of life is so dangerous for American African children.

The consequences of mortality rates ultimately translate into significantly lower life expectancy for American African males. Currently, the worst place to live in the United States if you are a black male is Washington, DC, where my brothers live an aver-

CHART 2: BLACK AND WHITE MALE INFANT MORTALITY RATES IN THE UNITED STATES, 1980–1996

Year	Black Males	White Males	% Higher BM/WM
1980	24.2	12.1	200%
1982	22.5	11.1	202%
1984	20.7	10.4	199%
1986	20.9	9.9	211%
1988	20.0	9.4	212%
1990	19.6	8.5	230%
1992	18.4	7.7	238%
1994	17.5	7.2	243%
1996	16.0	6.7	238%

Source: *National Vital Statistics Report*, Vol. 47, No. 9, November 10, 1998.

age of only 64.88 years. That places Washington, DC, at about the same level as men who grow up in Russia (64.7) and Pakistan (65.5) and lower than men who live in North Korea (67.0 years) and Bolivia (68.1 years). Ironically, Washington, DC, has the *highest* rate of life expectancy for white men (82.07).

But it gets worse. Even though the average life expectancy for American men is 78.74, black men live an average of 72.29 years yet there are 35 states where the life expectancy rate for them is below 70. The state that enjoys the highest life expectancy rate for black men is North Dakota (89.97 years), with New Hampshire following close behind with 85.56 years. Outside of the District of Columbia, Louisiana has the lowest life expectancy rate for black men, at 65.62 years.

While these statistics are sobering, they also engender anger

CHART 3: SELECTED INFANT MORTALITY RATES FOR VARIOUS COUNTRIES

Country	Infant Mortality Rate
Japan	6
Sweden	6.4
Switzerland	7.5
France	8.2
Singapore	8.8
United States (WHITE)	9.4
Italy	11.4
Greece	14.1
Cuba	15.0
United States (BLACK)	18.4

Source: World Health Organization.

among black men and women. Black children simply have no business dying twice as fast as white children, and black male infant mortality rates should be going down, not up. At the most superficial level, these data reflect the persistence of racism in one of the two most fundamental life journeys that all of us make—birth (the other being death)—and indicate the low value that America places on black males.

Turning again to Washington, DC, the black male's life expectancy is comparable to that of the entire U.S. population in 1920. This eighty-year lag in my brothers' life expectancy compared to the rest of the nation will worsen during the present century. If current trends continue, by 2100, while the average life expectancy for all Americans will approach one hundred years, black men will live only about as long as contemporary Americans—seventy-five years.

One could view these appalling data as support for the notion that black boys suffer from genetic inferiority. While such a racist notion lacks support, it is interesting to note rarely cited

CHART 4: MALFORMATIONS BY RACE PER 10,000 BIRTHS

Malformation	Blacks	Whites
Anencephaly	1.80	1.98
Spina bifida without anencephaly	1.74	2.00
Cleft palate without cleft lip	4.00	6.10
Cleft lip without cleft palate	4.40	9.70
Clubfoot	19.90	27.50
Down's syndrome	6.50	8.50

Source: *Health Status of Minorities and Low-Income Groups,* Third Edition, p. 106.

data comparing birth defects among American African children with those of their white counterparts. The infrequency of such studies could be construed as a fear of white neonatologists and other health researchers to discuss how genetic factors and race interact in the biological development of black and white children. Blacks are consistently lower than whites in nearly all categories of birth defects. Chart 4 illustrates selected malformations at birth by race. These statistics illustrate that black male infants are not dying because of genetic anomalies but because of environmental stressors—all of which are preventable. The conspiratorial silence on comparative birth defects among boys is related to the health care industry having to point a finger at itself for its negligence in providing adequate health care for black males.

Black Boys at Birth

Though starting life with a less-than-average chance of surviving the first year, black male babies can be protected even before birth to make their first life passage easier. With the first announcement of pregnancy, mothers should establish a group or a Birthing Circle that will provide the support and care to ensure a trouble-free pregnancy and birth. If the mother-to-be is married, her husband should be included in the circle. If single, the mother should look to both male and female relatives and friends for the community birthing. To some degree, this already occurs in families *informally*. I suggest a far more formalized structure that would include specific assignments to members of the circle. These circles should have between seven and ten persons and should be balanced with both men and women. Assignments within the Birthing Circle should include everything from pre- to postnatal care and support to home care for the expectant mother. The structure of the circle should involve the following:

Designating a person to monitor the mother's prenatal care, i.e., making sure that appointments are kept and accompanying her on doctor visits during the pregnancy. As previously stated, the infant mortality rate for black boys is preventable if proper prenatal care becomes a habit starting at conception. The Birthing Circle ensures that, at conception, a village is created that will guarantee that the mother has a strong support system for her child. Assigning a relative or an elder to accompany the expectant mother to her ob/gyn helps to foster good medical habits in the mother.

Designating a person (male or female) to join the mother for prenatal Lamaze, nutrition, or exercise classes. Much has been written about the "naturalness" of birth, even though physicians view it as a medical procedure. A circle member can explore with the mother the widely used Lamaze method, other holistic techniques such as Leboyer's birth without violence system, and midwifery while simultaneously educating her about the birthing process. A mother-to-be needs to follow a balanced diet throughout her pregnancy, and a circle member should assist with her nutrition education if necessary. Circle members should discourage the use of harmful products such as liquor and tobacco. Finally, the mother-to-be should keep a "diet diary" whenever possible, so that her closest friend or relative can make sure that she is receiving the nutrition both she and her baby need.

Designating a person to serve as a backup for completing the paperwork associated with childbirth. This includes health insurance, medical records, and paperwork required by either a midwife or hospital. The blizzard of paperwork associated with pre- and postnatal care, as well as birth itself, should not be a frustration for the mother. A circle member should assist so that unexpected expenses, insurance inquiries, and bills do not occupy a lot of her time.

Designating a person to serve as an information specialist on such things as naming, postbirth ceremonies, and health information. This should be a person acquainted with rites-of-passage ceremonies and African-centered naming ceremonies. Since Birthing Circles by design are African-centered, many persons can participate in this. The traditional "baby shower" can be supplemented with discussions about names, birth ceremonies, and spiritual matters associated with birth.

Designating a person to accompany the mother into the delivery room. This last point is very critical. The most obvious person to attend the birth of the child is the father, but often this is not an option. In that case, a family member or a close male friend should be with the mother at the time of delivery. None of these suggestions presuppose the "helplessness" of the black mother, nor do Birthing Circles have anything to do with Western notions of "sexism." They are, rather, the earliest expression of the male/female participation in the child's life and should accompany the baby from the day of conception.

Before delivery, friends and relatives should throw an African-centered baby shower. Books, clothing, music, and other items may be added to the traditional gifts of diapers, formula, and other baby supplies. Members of the Birthing Circle should attend this gathering, and visit at the time of delivery.

Naming Our Children

The increased popularity of giving black children African/Arabic names is a positive sign of our increasing consciousness of our African pasts. My own children—Omari Lateef, Sharifa Hasin, and Faraji Khalid—all have names meaningful to them that my wife and I chose carefully to reflect our hopes and aspirations for their lives. The name of my oldest son, Omari Lateef, means "high and gentle." His mother and I wanted him to be successful and fair in what he does. He is now a practicing attorney. The name Sharifa Hasin, my only daughter, means "nobly beautiful," and recognizes that we wanted her to be strong and charismatic in the work she does. She is in dental school. The name of my youngest son, Faraji Khalid, means "he will bring us peace," and while he and I have doubted that at times, his mother and I felt he came at a time of great stress in our lives, so his name reflects our hopes. West African naming ceremonies are important and sacred; the naming of a child is a major event among various clans and groups.

We must name our children with the utmost care and in a calm and meditative fashion. Too often, parents name children *phonetically*, rather than *culturally*, which results in meaningless names and bizarre spellings. Comedians can joke about many of these names because the naming has been done in the White Way. "Judahrusalem," "Lamonakeesha," and "Baramalooma," though phonetically pleasing, supply little information to the black child as to who he or she is. While it is not automatic that a child named Rolaqueesha will grow up confused about her racial identity, the most basic indicator given to a child, other than gender, should not be done in a haphazard or uninformed way.

Early Hurdles for Black Boys

The first two years of a black boy's life are fraught with dangers. After birth, black boys frequently lack adequate health care. Chart 5 indicates the persistence of mortality beyond birth among black male children. We will find that there is only one age range during which black males outlive their white counterparts—eighty-five years and older. Why black octogenarians live longer than their white peers is still unknown, but research could give valuable insight into this anomaly.

The Birthing Circle should continue through the newborn's first year of life. Members should encourage the mother to make sure that all scheduled immunizations take place; this is another area where black males fall short. The Birthing Circle should also encourage the mother to exercise and regain her prepregnancy figure; many black women report that after their pregnancy it is difficult to care for their newborn child and adhere to a diet and exercise routine.

Everyone in the Birthing Circle should read to the infant during the first year of his life. Music should also play an important role in the young child's development. Exposure to stimulating music, such as soft jazz and West African pieces, can attune his young mind to appreciate a variety of music in later years. New research also shows that infant massage and other forms of touch play a major role in the development and socialization

CHART 5: INFANT, NEONATAL, AND POSTNEONATAL MORTALITY RATES IN MALES, 2012

(Rates are [infant <1 year], [neonatal <28 days], [postneonatal 28 days to 11 months] per 100,000)

	Infant	Neonatal	Postneonatal
Black Males	12.33%	8.04%	4.29%
White Males	5.50%	3.71%	1.79%

Source: *National Vital Statistics Reports,* Vol. 63, No. 9, August 31, 2015.

of children. While infant massage is still quite common among West African cultures, it has all but disappeared among Africans in America. Black boys, in particular, need to be touched and held so that they develop a sense of openness in their relationships with others, particularly girls and women.

The spring of a young black male's life can be best described as stormy. But the dangers can be minimized if simple precautionary and preventative steps are taken. We will see in the following chapters how the remaining seasons of our sons' lives also contain dangers that can be prevented. Joseph Cinque was faced with similar odds when he was kidnapped from his homeland during the spring of 1839. He faced dangers while in the hull of the ship, during his captivity, and even as he journeyed back to his home in Sierra Leone. His children can overcome similar dangers if they are surrounded by parents, teachers, friends, and relatives who truly care about their well-being.

6

The Seasons of Our Sons: Summer, Ages 5–12

No one sends a child on a difficult errand and gets angry if he does not perform it well.

—ASHANTI PROVERB

Ages 5–12: Chad

I was in the middle of my psychology internship at the notorious Robert Taylor Homes (demolished in 2007) on Chicago's Southside. They were indeed "projects" since they seemed an "experimental" way of imprisoning their occupants in gloomy twenty-story buildings, with depressing fenced-in breezeways that prevented accidental or intentional falls to the debris-laden concrete sidewalks below. I chose the internship because I had been raised in a similar neighborhood, and I felt that my experiences growing up on the east side of Cleveland would benefit the children I was to see.

The decrepit elevators, reeking of urine, were dangerous places to be, and most of the residents avoided them when possible. Only the foolish rode them alone. The Head Start children to whom I was assigned were all housed on the first floor, which was clean and very well kept by a staff dedicated to the children in their care. I saw children in their classroom and in their homes. Most of the knowledge I had gained in my clinical psychology classes at the University of Chicago was better left at the doors of the apartments; almost none of it had any relevance to either the children or the adults there.

I saw whoever wanted to see me, despite the injunction of my professor to "focus" on the children in the Head Start program. I ignored his advice because there was a desperate need for mental health services in many of the tenants. I knew I was violating the strict rules of my future profession by counseling the residents, but I also knew that no one at Robert Taylor Homes cared about this. I supplied what counseling I could with the limited resources at my disposal. I continued in this way for several months; I helped parents develop study habits in their children, men to get jobs, boys to get their first jobs, and adolescents to cultivate an interest in museums and other educational facilities. Rumor spread quickly that a "cool" psychologist was seeing children there, and over the course of the semester-long internship, I saw children, adolescents, and adults suffering from the posttraumatic stresses of living in the dangerous, overcrowded conditions of the homes. It was apt that the horror film *Candyman* would later be set in Cabrini-Green, not far from these homes; monsters haunted these breezeways and elevators in the form of drug addiction, alcoholism, abuse, and homicide.

One day, the teachers and I decided to take the children for a long walk down State Street, something that many of the children did not get to do on a regular basis. As we were exiting the cavernous quadrangle of buildings, we saw a strange sight on the vandalized playground about fifty yards from the Head Start office. There, on the nearly broken-down swing set, was a beautiful young mother laughing wildly and swinging so hard that she was nearly parallel to the bars high above her head. The pathological environment she was in contrasted with her stunningly beautiful twenty-something face, which seemed strangely twisted above her threadbare winter coat. What captured our attention, however, was the little boy who was screaming and clinging desperately to her coat in fear of being flung out of her lap and onto the pavement.

Swinging up and down, she seemed to be carrying on a conversation with unseen people. I ran over to the swing, trying to figure out how I could get them both down without harm. I was afraid to grab the swing from behind, worried that its momentum would throw the little boy away from his mother. Instead, I went to the front of the swing and asked the mother to slow down or her child would fall. She looked at me, laughed, said "No!" then propelled the swing even higher. Her uncontrolled laughter, disheveled look, and conversation with voices no one else could hear made it obvious that she was a deinstitutionalized mental patient, who had fallen through the ever-widening human service cracks.

I asked her why she was swinging so high with her son, and she said that she "had to teach him early that the world was a hard place to live in and that he had to be hard in order to survive." I asked her what her son's name was, and she screamed "Chad!" Then she yelled at him to hold on real tight. For a split second I thought about the evils of a world that taught such harsh lessons so early in life. I yelled out to her that there were other ways to teach such lessons; my fellow teachers hollered that she could kill her child if she didn't come down immediately. Enjoying the attention, she swung even higher toward the sky and she laughed aloud at us. I told my companions to surround the swing in order to maximize our chances of catching the hysterical little boy in case he fell.

I stationed myself in front of the swing, ready to catch it as it soared above my head. Suddenly the young mother screamed, "That's enough for today!" and began to bring her maniacal swinging to a halt. As quickly as was safe, I grabbed her terrified son, who now held me even tighter than he had his mother. The women with me immediately got on her case, and the children from the Head Start class watched the entire episode. They asked her if she was crazy; the woman nodded assent and assured them that she was. Stepping in, I asked her why she felt it necessary to put her son's life in danger. I asked her if she had meant what she said while she was up in the air, and she said she had. She calmly replied that no one but *she* could teach her son how bad the world was, and that, had she been swung like that when she was small, she wouldn't have "wound up in a mental institution." This young mother thought that her son's experience on the swing would teach him that feeling good could often wind up making him feel bad.

This is what had happened to her. She then *asked* me if she could hold her son, and while I had no right to keep him from her, I hesitated until Chad turned from me and opened his arms to his mother. I gently handed him to her and watched as she hugged him closely. They both started laughing and crying. I told her to stop by the Head Start office and visit me. She nodded, but I knew that I would never see her or her son again.

That incident haunted me for years. I cannot walk past a playground without being reminded of that cool spring day. What has truly haunted and saddened me is that she was right. "America wasn't gonna give Chad any breaks in anything." Since that day I have witnessed often just how right she was.

Massaging the Numbers

The polished and sophisticated statistics of the performance of black boys in elementary and middle school ignore the violence that confines them to a statistical netherworld inhabited by uncaring teachers, bloated bureaucracies, and violent upbringings. American African boys have been endangered since they were first stolen from the shores of Africa nearly five centuries ago. In *On the Origin of Species by Means of Natural Selection*, Charles Darwin said, "If the differences among human beings is not due to biology but to our institutions then great is our sin." In other words, either black boys are *genetically* predisposed to commit crimes, sell drugs, and become fathers early on, or there is something seriously wrong with the institutions through which they move from birth to adulthood.

One of the most remarkable surprises about black boys is that their academic performance through the first four years of school is fairly good. Since 1969, the National Assessment of Educational Progress (NAEP), commonly referred to as the "nation's report card," has been the standard by which educational achievement by race and gender is measured. Though large gaps exist among the various students measured at fourth-, eighth-, and twelfth-grade levels, the 2015 scores of black students are very different from those of 1998. It is encouraging to note that at grade four, significant increases occurred for black students whose average reading score in 2015 was higher than in 1998. What is more interesting, however, is research on why achievement levels for black boys are so low.

Jason Osborne's 2006 study comparing black, white, and Latino achievement found that black boys experience an "emotional withdrawal" from academics at a greater rate than do whites or Latinos. Black boys exhibiting intellectual prowess are often teased by peers, due to a cultural emphasis on macho behavior. An environment that does not encourage intellectual growth often supports boys' emotional disengagement from school. Parents not participating in school meetings, peers who have weak academic goals, and uncaring teachers are ingredients in the educational crucible that obviates effective learning. A curious finding in the study, however, is that even though the grades of these boys plummeted, the psychological protocols used to measure their self-esteem remained the same over the four years and in some cases actually increased. Claude Steele, a black psychologist at Stanford, found similar results. He points out that powerful stereotypes over "being smart" in the African American community trigger anxiety and academic withdrawal on the part of black youngsters, particularly young black males in late elementary and middle school. Over the years I have seen many black boys in these grades ridiculed and deemed "less masculine" for earning good grades. These boys often struggle between making good grades and being accepted by friends who see good grades as "acting white." "Let's get stupid" is more than a phrase uttered on the dance floor. Jawanza Kunjufu and other educators have written about the false macho, encouraged by black boys' peers at ever-decreasing ages, which rewards brawn and discourages brains.

Even though Herculean efforts have been made during the past ten years on presenting the realities of paid athletic competition as an opportunity for American African boys, there are powerful incentives that dissuade them from believing these odds. Academic achievement falls even lower in the ranks when you add hip-hop culture's powerful influence, which often but

CHART 6: NAEP WRITING SCORES BY RACE AND GRADE, 2015

(Scale = 0–500)

Ethnic Group	Grade 4
White	232
Black	206
Latino	208
Asian/Pacific Islander	239
American Indian	205

	Grade 8
White	274
Black	248
Latino	253
Asian/Pacific Islander	280
American Indian	252

	Grade 12
White	295
Black	266
Latino	276
Asian/Pacific Islander	297
American Indian	279

Source: National Association of Educational Progress (NAEP), reading, mathematics, and writing scores. Accessed through the NAEP data explorer at https://nces.ed.gov/nationsreportcard/about/naeptools.aspx

not always encourages black macho behavior at the expense of academic achievement. It is ironic that since 1981, when Grand-master Flash and the Furious Five's powerful lyrics in "The Message" described an urban world in which there was resistance to the temptation of "going under," much of rap has abandoned its political roots and become highly commercialized. J. Cole, Kendrick Lamar, and A Tribe Called Quest are notable exceptions to this, but the signifying that took place during the mid-1990s represented in the deaths of Tupac Shakur and Biggie Smalls had a lasting impact on the image of hip-hop. Parents should listen to rap while they encourage their children to listen to artists who still bring a powerful message of political awareness and African-centered consciousness to their music.

I believe that the sharp decline in American African boys' academic achievement is due to factors associated with their transition into puberty. Along with peer pressure to perform athletically, there is a disturbing yet rarely discussed issue at work in the disregard for and stigma attached to a black boy who excels academically.

The late black psychologist Charles Thomas was the first to discuss how the sexual development of young black males threatens their mostly white and female teachers. Thomas argued that the societal taboo against black male/white female sexuality creates apprehension in white females, to the point that they fear its emergence in the black boys they teach.

Keep in mind that the primary instructors of black elementary and middle school boys are white females; the dynamics of this relationship are rarely investigated in trying to understand the decline in standardized test scores among pubescent black males. On more than one occasion, I have heard white female teachers refer to ten- to twelve-year-old black boys as "lady killers," "sexy," and "drop-dead gorgeous"—labels that go far beyond boosting self-esteem. On one occasion, after I conducted a workshop with teachers from a southern metropolitan area, a young white instructor approached me and said that she had a "crush" on one of her students. She looked to be in her mid-twenties, and I asked her what grade she taught. Meekly, she said, "Fifth." I asked her who the boy was, and she said that he was an eleven-year-old black boy. I was both shocked and angry and asked her how this was influencing her work with him. She told me that she tried to "avoid" him as much as possible, and that she was doing her best to "stay out of his way." I asked her if she thought her behavior and attitude were hurting him academically. She said they were, and that was why she was seeking advice. I told her that she needed to examine herself to find out what motivated her feelings. She thanked me and walked away hurriedly, seemingly ashamed of what she had just told me.

Though anecdotal, I believe that unconscious sexuality is a neglected factor in understanding the dramatic decline of academic success. It should be added to the list of "explanatory factors" influencing black boys' academic performance, which has included genes, poverty, nutrition, parenting, and poor academic preparation.

While we have seen recent scandals involving older female teachers raping young boys, little has been done to measure this taboo subject across racial lines; the research would have to rely on self-reported data and would, of course, involve minors. I have spoken to other black educators about this subject, and many of them tell how they have overheard white female teachers talk in sexual terms about their black male students. The sexual anxiety felt by many of these teachers could easily translate into rejection and avoidance of their pubescent black male students. As stated earlier, the fascination with black sexuality has a long history in America; even though it is a difficult topic, its discussion would shed light on many issues.

Violence, Health, and Athletics

Separating violence from health issues is impossible when talking about young black boys. According to a 2014 Centers for Disease Control and Prevention study of the ten leading causes of death among males in the United States, homicide ranks fourth (4.3 percent of all deaths) among black males and only ranks in two other groups, Latinos (2.3 percent) and American Indians (2.1 percent). Simultaneously, black males are the only ethnic group in the United States where suicide is *not* in the top ten causes of death. Guns consistently remain the weapons of choice among black males with thirty-four deaths per one hundred thousand compared to sixteen per one hundred thousand white males.

In 1992, the Centers for Disease Control and Prevention (CDC) argued empirically that violence is a public health problem, and ignited a firestorm of response when it declared that handguns were directly connected to the high incidence of homicidal violence in the United States, particularly among young American African males. The report viewed handguns, like cigarettes, as a "health hazard" and was prophetic in predicting that both industries would be sued because of the danger they posed to Americans.

If it sounds like a litmus test, it is. Handguns are the primary instrument of death for young black boys. The gun has become romanticized among American African communities in films and music. This insidious blend of guns and media poses a health hazard for black boys during the summer and fall years of their lives (ages five through eighteen). During these years, the social pressures placed in black boys' paths begin to "show" them how American society expects them to act. The lessons taught are that violence, athleticism, and entertainment are their *primary* choices in life. In this section I will discuss the importance of providing a counterbalance to the harmful and misleading images and messages from the all-powerful media. Media educates children *and* socializes them, and part of this socialization involves how children perceive persons from different racial and ethnic backgrounds. When adolescents watch television and other visual media, they are strongly influenced by the racial and gender stereotypes presented to them. Not much has changed since Manuel Alvarado, Robin Gutch, and Tana Wollen found in 1987 that black characters on television are usually portrayed in four different ways: exotic, dangerous, humorous, and pitiable. Although American Africans appear more frequently on television than they once did, a 1990 seminal study by Gerbner, Gross, Morgan, and Signorielli, of the Universities of Pennsylvania and Massachusetts, found that they are often depicted negatively, as criminals or victims of violent crimes. *Atlantic Monthly* has dubbed Gerbner the "Man Who Counts the Killings," and his Annenberg Center research is rigorous and well documented. Known mostly for documenting how many murders children watch by the time they are twelve, Gerbner has meticulously coded the presence and images of all ethnic groups and both genders on television for years.

What has changed significantly since that major study of ethnic images on television is the advent of social media on the Internet. YouTube, WorldstarHipHop, and Facebook are all sites where intraracial violence is readily available at the click of a mouse to children of all ages and races. Added to the fact that now nearly everyone has a camera via their telephone, and it makes for a deadly mix of internalizing violence at an early age, especially among black children who consume all forms of media at higher rates than whites. More will be said about this in my later chapter entitled "Barack Obama, and Other Victims of White Supremacy."

Nearly twenty years ago (1999) the National Association for the Advancement of Colored People (NAACP) issued scathing indictments of the networks for the lack of people of color on their prime-time shows. The networks responded to this charge by introducing new characters and expanding the roles of black, Latino, and Asian actors in their evening shows. While the nation's leading civil rights organizations should sustain such political pressure, they should place additional emphasis on encouraging parents of black children to alter their viewing habits altogether; black children, particularly boys, watch far too much television. The expectation that adding a few ethnic characters to prime-time network television will reverse the damage already done by a medium that has been a primary shaper of negative ethnic images sounds like a compromise rather than a comprehensive solution. Raising Warriors must include implementing realistic strategies to educate black boys on how media manipulates their images. Teachers and parents can structure "no-TV nights" and replace them with individual and group activities that foster a positive self-image.

At the turn of the present century, educators decried the gap between blacks and whites on the "information highway." Terms like *digital divide* were widely used to decry how blacks and Latinos were lagging behind whites in access to technology and the Internet. There were dire predictions that not having access to this information highway was going to widen the educational gap between blacks and whites, particularly in K–12. These predictions were wrong because they failed to predict three things: 1) the mainstream success of the smartphone in 2007, 2) the drop in computer prices between 1995 and 2005, and 3) the advent of social media. Regardless of the motives behind why these studies were conducted in the first place, capitalism triumphed in making available computers and ways of accessing the Internet. The primary technological discussions after 2010 centered around broadband access especially as it related to rural areas both in the United States and abroad. As an educator, I have always been cynical about producing "ten-to-twenty-year" "predictive" studies on the future of education since it is rare that any of them include unanticipated developments that will alter nearly every "recommendation" produced by the reports. For example, imagine that you are a school superintendent in 1990 and you assemble a panel to provide a report on the educational goals and objectives for your school district for 2010. You give it a futuristic title like "Predictions About Education in Smalltown: 1990–2010." If the report is conducted and doesn't wind up on a dusty shelf in your office, it will not contain the words *Internet* and *broadband*, two inventions that revolutionized how children learn during the past twenty years.

The investigative and inquisitive behavior associated with information technology should be cultivated at younger ages and can be a project for Birthing Circles that can continue to provide educational support for the child as he enters the summer of his life. Since 2000, cooperative computer purchases took place in black neighborhoods around the country, and civic and religious groups contributed to these purchases as part of their outreach to these communities so that their residents would have access to these technologies.

Over thirty years ago, in 1985, I was instrumental in establishing the Computer Institute for Teaching Youth (CITY) in the Preston Taylor Homes, a public housing project in Nashville. For a leasing fee of $1 per year, the local housing authority allowed us to renovate a burned-out unit and convert it into an after-school program of linked and now extinct Acorn Computers, thanks to a generous donation from United Press International to be used for staff and computers. This was at the dawn of the computer age, but the twelve machines were fairly powerful for that time; they became an instant hit among the residents as entertainment, education, and research tools.

Because parents were just as fascinated with the machines, we expanded the services and offered adult classes in word processing and spreadsheet management. A club called I Believe in Myself (IBIM for short) was started for boys and girls in their summer years, and was done purely to enhance the self-esteem of the children. Attendance was mandatory in order to work on the computers, and the students rarely missed a class. We taught the children about the rich scientific contributions of such persons as Charles Drew, Lewis Latimer, Mae Jemison, and other black scientists who distinguished themselves in many areas.

The teachers in the program were excited about the flexibility they had in teaching, and the children loved it all. Though it lasted only two years, its impact was substantial and far ranging. And no one even missed television during the classes.

More recently, the Internet has served as one of the best tools for organizing and educating people about events in the American African community. We forget that the 1995 Million Man March was the first major event using the Internet as an organizing tool. Similar publicity would be used to draw attention to cases involving Mumia Abu-Jamal, Abner Louima, and Amadou Diallo. Later, social media brought global attention to what Africans in America had been discussing for over a century: police brutality and killings of black men and women. Trayvon Martin, Michael Brown, Sandra Bland, and Philando Castile all proved that the use of social media was a powerful tool in the hands of black folk. In the work I do, I find that young black males in their summer years are eager to work on computers and that this eagerness can be useful in teaching learning skills in reading, writing, and mathematics.

Blacks should think of the technological gap as *partially* a self-help project. The affordability of computers today actually makes it more cost-effective to own a computer than not; renting computer time or traveling to facilities that have free computer access is time-consuming. Furthermore, purchasing goods over the Internet can also save money that would otherwise be spent at traditional brick-and-mortar stores. Educators, policy makers, and parents could mount a "Marshall Plan" to ensure

CHART 7: PERCENT OF HOMES HAVING COMPUTERS BY ETHNICITY

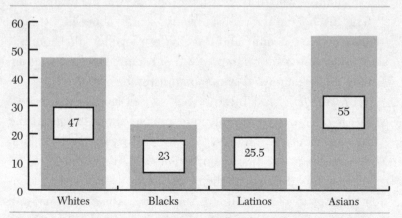

Source: U.S. Commerce Department, 1999 Report, "Falling Through the Net."

that by 2025 this technological gap will be eliminated and that the Young Warriors in their summer years can continue to beat the electronic drum. It can begin with all black organizations—civic, professional, and religious—purchasing and donating ten fully equipped state-of-the-art computers to black families each year for the next ten years.

Conservatively, this could place a hundred thousand computers in black homes each year, and over a million by the year 2025. The donation program should include payment for one year of Internet access and maintenance contracts with vendors until each family is familiar with the basic maintenance of the system.

Black organizations can decide for themselves how the ten computers can be distributed, perhaps through contests, raffles, or incentive programs. Some organizations will be able to place more, but none should place less than ten per year. This program will do much to aid African American families to keep pace with the technological revolution currently under way.

Mental Health and Black Boys

When the mental health of black boys is discussed, it usually focuses on two areas: intelligence and violence. From saliva to bell curves, the physiological analysis of black males creates the impression of a genetic predisposition to violence and a lack of intelligence. Shortly after Hillary Clinton declared that inner-city youth were "superpredators" in 1996, the University of Chicago in 1999 reported a widely cited study in which cortisol, a stress hormone, was noticeably low in the saliva of aggressive boys between the ages of seven and twelve. Though the study had only thirty-eight subjects, it was seen as a "breakthrough" in understanding how to treat violent youth; one of the researchers, Keith McBurnett, concluded, "Perhaps what we're dealing with here is a biological propensity that's resistant to treatment, which is very troubling. The implication is that we may need to discard our traditional notions of treatment with these kids in favor of trying to help them fit in and find a niche in society where their aggressiveness and lack of a sense of danger is an asset." Once again, black males as inferior and aggressive is suggested. If aggressive behavior is biological, as this terribly flawed study suggests, then it stands to reason that black boys in their summer years are hopelessly unresponsive to counseling and other interventions.

Robert Guthrie, in his book *Even the Rat Was White,* shows how the patterns of making young black children feel inferior have been a part of "scholarly" research since the beginning of educational investigations in this country. While most social scientists consider themselves free of racist worldviews, James Scheurich and Michelle Young argued in *Educational Researcher* that "epistemological racism" pervades the research involving persons of color. They opine that it arises out of racism's domination of society, and that a "white" worldview is simply taken for granted by most scientists. The denial that a "white worldview" exists among most white scientists manifests itself when journals not accepted "by the mainstream" are viewed with contempt by those who evaluate black scholars for tenure. This epistemological racism forces black scholars to adopt strategies for surviving the academy that opposes what they may actually know to be true about black populations. Publishing the "right stuff," or what one of my colleagues refers to

as the "white stuff," is a necessary strategy for gaining tenure at
most traditionally white universities. This biased research justified the enslavement of black people, preserved the notion that
racial segregation was the best way to educate all children, and
supported the idea that white genetic pools would be contam-
inated with the addition of intellectually inferior black blood.
The invention of the "intelligence test" forced psychology to
give up its political virginity and began the consignment of black
children to lower educational castes. Guthrie cites the infamous
early-twentieth-century crusade of Stanford University psychologist Lewis Terman, who convinced several state legislatures to sterilize men, women, and children who were deemed
"moronic" based on intelligence test data. Over ten thousand
persons were sterilized during the Terman years, with many of
them poor, black, developmentally disabled, and consigned to
the netherworld of state mental hospitals.

While black violence and genetic inferiority seem to dominate the comparative literature between black and white boys,
what is rarely discussed is the difference in mental health issues
between these two groups. Random schoolyard shootings and
white-on-white crime have recently illuminated the instability
of white boys' mental health. The Centers for Disease Control
notes that:

> Current data confirms previous research that showed a
> differential vulnerability to psychological disorders for
> boys as compared with girls. . . . Several researchers sug-
> gest that boys' greater susceptibility to such problems may
> be explained by a greater vulnerability to psychosocial
> stressors in their environments, such as family conflict,

divorce and parental psychopathology. . . . Moreover, according to parental reports, higher proportions of white children have had one or more of these disorders than Asian or black children. . . .

The study also said,

It is surprising that the prevalence of these disorders was not higher for minority children because black and Hispanic families have several characteristics that suggest they are at risk for higher rates of psychological disorders. [Italics added]

This is an important finding despite the fact that the researchers seem surprised that black and Latino children do not suffer from mental disorders as much as their white peers. Similar to the reaction to the higher incidence of birth defects among white infants, there seems to be a reluctance to discuss the psychological problems associated with being young, white, and male. Violence continues to be associated with being young and black, despite the frequency of the mass shootings perpetrated by white boys in recent years. Parents, educators, and anyone involved with black boys need to understand such information to counterbalance the negative image of black boys during their summer years.

Young Warrior Councils

In recent years, Boys and Girls Clubs, the Boy Scouts, and several other organizations have become more "culturally sensitive" to the needs of our sons. The Boy Scouts of America, for example, now gives a merit badge for "crime prevention," indicating its "cultural awareness" that some of its members live in high-crime areas. Nearly all of these organizations have Black History Month programs, recognize the birthday of Martin Luther King Jr., and in some cases celebrate Kwanzaa. At best, however, these activities are grafted onto the association's programs. They are peripheral rather than central to the needs of the black boys within the organization. What black boys need are clubs and organizations that are culturally specific to them.

The Birthing Circle should continue until the boy is five years old, at which time he should be inducted into a Young Warrior Council. These clubs are modeled on the Poro Societies of West Africa.

Poro Societies removed their initiates from their homes so that they would be immersed in their training. The boys memorized the history and laws of their clan and of surrounding clans. One of the more accurate moments of the terribly flawed 1997 film *Amistad* was Cinque's helping in his own legal defense. This was a core teaching of Poro students—learn and understand the law of others as well as your own. Boys learned the medicinal properties of plants for a range of ailments, and studied the literature of their clan and other great legendary traditions of West Africa. They learned as many languages as they could, again reflected in Cinque's relatively quick mastery of English before his trial.

The Young Warrior Councils expand from six months to eight years the time devoted to the boys' psychological, social, physical, and emotional development. This lengthy period is necessary because, unlike with Poro Society, black boys are returned to environments that hinder their development, not support it.

Protecting a child is different from *overprotecting* a child, and black boys remain vulnerable to racism as they mature more than white boys. The steps in creating a Young Warrior Council are outlined below. These ideas are based on work done with dozens of educators and thousands of black boys over a twenty-five-year period and published in a 2013 *Peabody Journal of Education* entitled "Hard Bigotry, Low Expectations and Soft Support: Educating American African Boys in the United States with the Warrior Method." I have deliberately made these steps flexible so that they can be adopted by a variety of organizations.

1. *The Birthing Circle established during pregnancy should surround the child until five years of age.* Birthing Circles should continue the attention given to the mother and child during pre- and postnatal care throughout the boy's spring years. Each Birthing Circle should be given a name including the area in which the mother lives, the street name, and her family name. For example, the Birthing Circle for the son of Mary Williams, who lives on Malcolm X Boulevard in Harlem, would be called: Harlem-Malcolm X/Williams Birthing Circle. Seven Birthing Circles together would compose a *clan,* which will help govern the lives of seven boys from conception to age five, and eventually will form the Young Warrior Council that takes over when the seven boys turn five. Birthing Circles can continue to "adopt" other women and boys who wish to be in them, and the members of the circle should keep detailed records of the women and children throughout the life of the child. This latter point is similar to Poro Societies, which kept meticulous records of past students so that the clan history could be passed down from generation to generation.

2. *At five years old, the boys begin the process of becoming*
   members of the Young Warrior Council. Seven boys should
   be inducted in a ceremony that announces their admittance
   to the council. The ceremony should be attended by as many
   family members as possible, during which the following program occurs:

   a. Pouring of libations to the ancestors. This ceremony has
      become increasingly popular at African-centered gath-
      erings; water is poured over a plant or directly on the
      ground to pay homage to the ancestors. Ironically, the
      use of liquor to do the same thing has become a popular
      means of paying tribute to "dead homies" in inner cities
      throughout the nation. Libations signify the connection
      of all African people in the *Maafa na Maangamizi*, and of
      the respect the living have for the dead, as well as for the
      unborn. It should be done by the oldest male and female
      present to symbolize the importance of both genders in
      the life of the Young Warrior.

   b. Greetings by the oldest woman in the Birthing Circle.
      After the libations are completed, the sacredness of the
      woman in African culture should be acknowledged with
      the oldest woman opening the program. This is a simple
      yet important announcement to the gathering that women
      give birth to the world, and that without them all life
      would cease. It also reminds the young boy that women
      are to be listened to and respected. Members of the Birth-
      ing Circle should review nostalgic incidents so that the
      young man can hear how his elders have cared for him
      since his conception.

   c. Greetings by the oldest man in the Birthing Circle. The
      presence of the elder man is important since it is a cere-

mony involving male initiation, and he should speak words concerning the importance of boys, and give a brief history of the Birthing Circle.

d. Reading of the *Nguzo Saba* (Seven Principles) by the mother of the boy. The widely known *Nguzo Saba* (pronounced nah-gu-ZSO SAH-bah), read by the mother to her son, emphasizes how these have been and should continue to be guiding principles in his life. Created by Maulana Karenga in 1965, the *Nguzo Saba* has found popularity among American Africans as the celebration of Kwanzaa becomes more widespread. Maulana Karenga stresses the importance of informality in its celebration. The principles, though elaborated on by several persons, are originally stated as follows:

1. *Umoja* (uu-MOH-jah) Unity: To strive for and maintain unity in the family, community, nation, and race.

2. *Kujichagulia* (KUU'-jee-chah-guu-lee-ah) Self-Determination: To define ourselves, name ourselves, create for ourselves, and speak for ourselves.

3. *Ujima* (uu-JEE'-mah) Collective Work and Responsibility: To build and maintain our community together and make our brother's and sister's problems our problems and to solve them together.

4. *Ujamaa* (UU'-jah-mah) Cooperative Economics: To build and maintain our own stores, shops, and other businesses and to profit from them together.

5. *Nia* (NEE'-ah) Purpose: To make our collective vocation the building and developing of our community in order to restore our people to their traditional greatness.

6. *Kuumba* (Ku-UUM'-bah) Creativity: To do always as much as we can, in the way we can, in order to leave our community more beautiful and beneficial than we inherited it.

7. *Imani* (eh-MAH'-NEE) Faith: To believe with all our heart in our people, our parents, our teachers, our leaders, and the righteousness and victory of our struggle.

e. Recitation of the *Nguzo Saba* by each of the seven boys being inducted. The seven boys repeat the reading of the *Nguzo Saba* for emphasis.

f. Gift by the oldest man of a strip of *Kente* cloth to each boy, which will signify his induction into the Young Warrior Council. *Kente* cloth has become symbolic of the beauty and strength of West African culture. The cloth is both beautiful and strong, and as each boy receives his strip, the elder should note its beauty and strength in relation to him. Just as European coats of arms are visible representations of a family's history, so *Kente* represents the culture, art, history, and folklore of clans in West Africa. The Young Warrior Council should adopt a *Kente* cloth, agreed upon by the elders, which reflects the boys within the council. Each cloth should be worn at appropriate gatherings and, when not in use, hung in a prominent place in the boy's bedroom.

g. Seven boys stand together while members of the Birthing Circle form an unbroken circle around them. The oldest man, the youngest man, the oldest woman, and the youngest woman in the Birthing Circle then offer prayers for the well-being of the boys as well as the members of the Birthing Circle. At the end of this ritual, the Birthing Circle is renamed the Young Warrior Council, and the seven Young Warriors are officially inducted.

h. All persons engage in a community feast (*karamu*), which consists of healthy food and no alcohol. Kwanzaa celebrations are also ended with a *karamu,* and the feast gives the boys and the members of the Young Warrior Council an opportunity to bond even further. Since there are minors present, no alcohol should be served, which also reminds the boys of the importance of avoiding substances harmful to the body.

The Birthing Circle has now become the Young Warrior Council and the boys, who are now five years old, should have several structured pursuits that prepare them for school.

3. The fifth year should include the following activities:

a. Monthly meetings for members of the Young Warrior Council and the seven Young Warriors should be informal and rotate among the homes of council members. The meetings, a continuation of the Birthing Circle, should supplement the education received by the boy in his formal schooling. Run on a rotating basis by the parents/guardians of each of the seven boys, meetings should begin by addressing council business.

Group activities, which should remain flexible, should center the boys' attention on their place in the adult world, and take into account the preferences of the adults and the boys.

b. Each of the seven Young Warriors should read three age-appropriate books during the first year. Reading should by now be a habit with the boys, and book selection should create group cohesiveness around a topic of interest. The boys should agree on the books they collectively read and discuss why they chose them. The elders in the council should guide the boys in selecting their books after listening to the boys' suggestions. On the web, African American Literature Book Club (AALBC) is an excellent place to select books for black children. Their list of 120 recommended black books for children is invaluable and is regularly updated (see: https://aalbc.com/books/children.php).

c. The newly formed Young Warrior Council should take field trips, discuss healthy living, and provide science instruction and lectures that teach the boys about African history and culture. Young Warrior Councils may choose to exchange information among themselves about supplemental education, but the burden of instruction for its boys should rest with each individual Young Warrior Council. Similar activities were conducted during Poro initiation, when boys were taught extensively about astronomy, agriculture, art, and music.

d. At the end of twelve months, the Young Warrior Council should conduct an agreed-upon ceremony that inducts the boys into their sixth year. No set ceremony is offered for this event; rather, it should be planned by all council members as an exercise in creativity. It should showcase what the Young Warriors have learned during the year.

4. The sixth year should repeat the basic curriculum of the fifth year, adding information technology as a key component of the learning process. While the addition of computers and the Internet can begin during the fifth year, it should be formalized when the boys turn six. The ubiquity of computers

does not automatically translate into computer literacy. The Young Warriors should be thoroughly familiar with the use of computers by the end of their sixth year. If adults within the council are weak in this area, they should involve themselves in learning about using new technology. If computers are unavailable in the homes of the council members, efforts should be made to hold a portion of the monthly meetings at a local library or other facility where Internet access is available. A group project may involve purchasing computers with a year's access to the Internet for each of the Young Warriors. Council elders should emphasize using technology to establish close ties with Africa and the *Maafa na Maangamizi*. Many resources exist on the Internet that make it easy to locate "pen pals" among African children, particularly in West, East, and South Africa. Spelling bees and oratorical contests should be held among the seven Young Warriors and their councils. Spelling bees are old-fashioned ways of honing spelling skills while having fun. A few years ago, I helped organize a spelling bee for a local civic group whose officers were skeptical about whether it would attract a large crowd. Each family of club members offered their best speller, and they were divided into appropriate age categories. Words were selected by a panel of three teachers who were members of the group. Prizes for each age group included a dictionary, a desk encyclopedia, a thesaurus, and a book on black history. Attendance was excellent at the event, and several people commented on how simple yet fun preparing for the contest was. It brought families closer together and rewarded good study habits. Oratorical contests, in which contestants select passages to recite and are then judged by a panel, are good ways of increasing the public-speaking ability of black children. Relatively easy events to organize, they can be held in churches or community centers. Debates are also in keeping with Poro Society initiation rites. All members of Poro Society were taught the importance of public speaking. Witnesses at the trial of Joseph Cinque noted his eloquence, even though he spoke with broken English, about his desire for freedom.

5. The seventh year begins the study of law and media. If the proper instruction has taken place during the first two years of the Young Warriors program, the seven Warriors will be prepared to analyze their self-image by understanding how the world sees them. The first six years of the boys' lives should be a time in which there is no lack of positive black male role models, something that psychologist Carolyn Murray of the University of California, Riverside, says is the most critical element of the development of self-image among black boys. The Young Warrior Councils should surround the boys with older black males who can mentor them and serve as their surrogate fathers in case no fathers are present in the boys' immediate families. They can help to teach the boys about how black males are perceived in media and how these perceptions begin when the boys are young. Black children watch a lot of television, teaching them to recognize how their images are manufactured, manipulated, and marketed is a critical learning experience for them.

The boys must also become familiar with the law, particularly laws related to arrest and incarceration. As previously stated, I am angry that I have to write this because of the numerous shootings involving police and black males. Trayvon Martin, Tamir Rice, Walter Scott, and Laquan McDonald are but a few of the dozens of black boys and men who have been shot in cold blood by police and self-styled vigilantes. Ideally, seven-year-old black boys should be focused on their education and the things that youngsters do at this age. Their environment should be relatively free from worries that they might be stopped and killed by police officers. This is not the case, however, and Young Warriors must learn simple lessons like these as they approach adolescence.

Classes should be held with workers in juvenile facilities, and attorneys who have experience with youth law should talk to the seven Warriors. They should talk frankly with boys about what happens to them if the police stop them. If possible, Young Warriors should visit juvenile courts to witness firsthand the legal process. Black boys are being criminalized at increasingly younger ages, and seven is not too young to hear why this is so.

The legal instruction should not be tedious; mock trials could acquaint the boys with the role of law-enforcement officers. Most local law schools and/or dedicated lawyers can help arrange legal instruction quite easily if approached by a conscientious group of parents wanting the best for their sons. Two mock trials that give roles to lawyers, judges, and juries can be held during the year. The National Bar Association is a good place to seek help in this effort.

Visits with responsible black police officers should be done carefully. Young Warriors and the members of the Warrior Council should question the police, particularly in the area of how law enforcement works in their neighborhood. In light of police homicides and brutality cases in the past few years, e.g., Freddie Gray here in Baltimore, I have found police departments eager to participate in events that invite them to discuss their work as law enforcers. Many cities have organized black police officer groups that are often at odds with their departments over the treatment of black citizens. A visit by officers on a twice-yearly basis, particularly just before winter vacation and summer vacation, is a good investment in the safety of black boys. These discussions should be frank, and only police officers who are willing to answer tough questions should make the presentation.

6. The seventh and eighth years should expand on what the Young Warriors have already learned, particularly in the areas of media and law. In addition, council members should be aware of negative images confronting black boys in entertainment. Older parents who disparage rap should understand that younger black males identify strongly with rap artists, and black parents and adults in the Young Warrior Council should be well acquainted with contemporary hip-hop artists such as Jay-Z, Drake, and Kendrick Lamar. There should be no "generation gap" between black adults and children regarding the music in our communities.

   Young Warrior Councils should also include an expanded curriculum centering on music and the arts of African people. Jazz and music from the *Maafa na Maangamizi* can be used to extend the listening range of the boys. Books such as *The New Grove Dictionary of Jazz* are extremely helpful in choosing music that can be used for *black* music appreciation classes. Young Warriors should hear classic jazz artists such as Jelly Roll Morton, Louis Armstrong, Billie Holiday, and Miles Davis; and council members who know about the history of jazz should hold lectures. Again, community resources should always be utilized if resources are not available within the council. If members of the circle lack extensive knowledge about the history of black American music, then they should find someone outside of the council to help.

It is particularly important that a history of black music be traced from Africa to America. Portia Maultsby's research at Indiana University on the evolution of black music styles is helpful in visualizing the history of music from both sides of the Atlantic. There should be a discussion on how Elvis Presley, the Rolling Stones, Eric Clapton, and others borrowed ("culturally appropriated") heavily from the blues tradition for their inspiration, teaching black boys to appreciate the influence their ancestors have had on music throughout the *Maafa na Maangamizi*. Analyzing the history of blues, gospel, jazz, rock and roll, rhythm and blues, soul, and rap will be fun for all in the council and at the same time infuse everyone with a positive sense of self and an appreciation of the cultural contributions of American Africans.

By this point, Young Warriors should be reading and discussing four books per year. Consulting reading lists from black bookstores and getting recommendations by word of mouth can help. Books should be discussed informally, and each boy should be encouraged to participate. If a hearing- or seeing-impaired boy is a Young Warrior, provisions should be made for interpreters or any other services to allow for his full participation. The adults in the council should ask questions that will spark discussions of the book by the boys. Haki Madhubuti's *Black Men: Obsolete, Single, Dangerous?* gives a list of two hundred books that all black people should read. This combined list provides a solid base for beginning a systematic reading of black life in the *Maafa na Maangamizi*. I hesitate to list a "canon" of black books, since I believe that individual Young Warrior Councils should develop their own reading lists relevant to the boys they are mentoring. Some children can understand books such as *Before the Mayflower*, which outlines the contributions of Africans to the ancient world, before others. What is exciting about a systematic reading program is that parents, teachers, and children are involved in lively discussions that will be mentally engaging and informative.

Field trips should be expanded to include concerts and other venues where black art is showcased. Many historically black colleges and universities (HBCUs) host regular groups of black middle and high school students from all over the country, giving tours of black campuses and historic sites in the South. These trips give visual connections to the sites where enslavement of our ancestors occurred and even more important sites where struggles against racism took place. Suggestions for places to visit can be found in George Cantor's *Historic Landmarks of Black America*. They should include the traditional visits to Martin Luther King's grave in Atlanta and also some of the following sites:

Vicksburg, Mississippi—slave auction sites
Sea Islands of Georgia—Gullah cultural historic sites
National Museum of African American History and
    Culture, Washington, DC
Tuskegee University, Tuskegee, Alabama—site of the
    laboratory of George Washington Carver
Fisk University—Aaron Douglas murals; histories of
    W. E. B. Du Bois, George Padmore, Nikki Giovanni,
    and the Fisk Jubilee Singers
Harlem, New York

Preservation Hall, New Orleans—"ground zero" for a
    history of jazz
Underground railroad stations, particularly in Ohio
DuSable Museum, Chicago—one of the best African
    American museums in the country
Piney Woods School, Piney Woods, Mississippi—one
    of the best secondary schools in the country with a
    history of black education to match
Southampton County, Virginia—site of the 1831 Nat
    Turner rebellion against enslavement
Nicodemus, Kansas—one of the oldest black settlements
    in America

This is a short list of historic places that are often passed
over for more popular sites. Money should never be a hin-
drance to exploring cultural sites within the community of the
Young Warrior Council. Black communities throughout the
United States have cultural histories that are often unknown
to their residents. Furthermore, several of these sites exist in
white neighborhoods, particularly in suburban areas that are
now predominantly white. Burial grounds of enslaved Africans were discovered in New York and in Nashville with neither in proximity to local black communities, and have been
fruitful in understanding the early cultural legacy of Africans
in America. Within the vicinity of each council, scavenger
hunts for historical documentation of black people's contri-
bution should be researched as the boys grow older. Parents
and council members can coordinate them. These can be
viewed as "sacred spaces" in our communities and would
provide places of visitation and meditation for our children.

7. The ninth and tenth years are critical in the development of Young Warriors. For most boys this is the fourth grade, when the assault on their psychological well-being begins in earnest. I have speculated earlier why these assaults intensify at the beginning of puberty, and it is important that the elders in the Warrior Council become vigilant in monitoring the institutions that are instructing their boys. Councils that have already established strong ties with the seven Young Warriors' school should strengthen these ties. The Council should make sure that parents attend all parent-teacher conferences and, when possible, should volunteer as teachers' aides in the Young Warriors' classrooms. Research is overwhelming that a close tie to the school by parents ensures good grades and strong attendance; this should be a primary concern of Young Warrior Councils.

   The seven Warriors should also be included in the ceremonies marking the induction of new Young Warriors. Their participation can consist of pouring libations or simply attending the ceremonies. During these special occasions, the boys should wear their *Kente* cloth strips, and their parents should encourage peer mentoring between the older and younger Warriors.

8. The eleventh and twelfth years are looking-ahead years for the rites-of-passage ceremony, celebrating the seven Young Warriors' turning thirteen. By now, they should be reading five books per year, have a broad understanding of their legal rights, have a worldview of African life, and have a firm understanding of computers and the Internet. The emphasis during these years is a strong education in savings and eco-

nomics. The seven Young Warriors may already be earning and managing money, but now the boys should be taught the global dimensions of money, economies, and thrift. How money can be used to strengthen black communities (*Ujamaa* in the *Nguzo Saba*) should be taught and encouraged. If they have not already done so, Young Warriors should open savings accounts in each of their names, preferably at a black financial institution.

It is also not too early to teach lessons in how Eurocentric institutions handle money. The Young Warriors and the councils can both benefit from learning how Wall Street and foreign financial markets operate to ensure that the institutions, corporations, and countries they represent stay strong and healthy, often at the expense of persons of color. Mock investment is a way of doing this, and friendly competition between Warrior Councils can be set up, with simulated investments on Wall Street. Various online trading sites such as etrade. com offer investment simulations that teach youngsters how the stock market works. Simulations should always be conducted with an eye toward teaching young men the importance of reinvesting their money within the African American community.

At a very real level, each council should begin an investment club where the Young Warriors' money, small though it may be, is invested to earn returns in cooperative ventures. The councils can advise the boys about investment possibilities, cooperative investment, and other projects that involve the money they have saved and lent to the club. Small contributions of $5 per week by each Young Warrior can result in an annual investment of over $1,800. Like other activities of the Young Warrior Council, advice should be taken from experts in the particular area of group interest. If available, black stockbrokers or any expert in long-term financial management can advise the group. The council should be particularly concerned about college tuition for the boys. Many states have government-run tuition plans to lighten the financial burden of parents sending children to college. Again, the council should base the amount of the investment on the economic level of its community. The group should unanimously agree upon the amount so that its financial goals can be met. The investment club should continue into the autumn years of the Young Warriors.

The goal of the investment clubs is not to encourage the materialism that characterizes much of the West, but to teach the boys about the system that influences so many young black men to sacrifice everything in the pursuit of money. Understanding how economies work and making them beneficial to American African communities should be the goal of the councils during this year. Niki Butler Mitchell's *The New Color of Success* is one of the few books that discusses young black entrepreneurs and how they acquired their money. What is refreshing about the book is that it *does not* include athletes and entertainers, and it provides a new array of young and rich black folk with goals that largely have to do with their commitment to African-centered values.

The end of the twelfth year marks the beginning of the rite of passage that will induct the seven Young Warriors into adulthood.

7

The Seasons of Our Sons:
Autumn, Ages 13–21

*I have told you all these things . . . because you are
my son, the eldest of my sons, and because I have
nothing to hide from you. There is a certain form
of behavior to observe, and certain ways of acting
in order that the guiding spirit of our race may
approach you also.*

—CAMARA LAYE, GUINEAN AUTHOR OF *THE BLACK CHILD*

The Notion of "Adolescence"

*I would there were no age between sixteen and three and
twenty, or that youth would sleep out the rest; for there is nothing in the between but getting wenches with child, wronging
the ancientry, stealing, fighting.*

—WILLIAM SHAKESPEARE, *THE WINTER'S TALE*, III, III

Adolescence is a nebulous Latin term that literally means "to be
nourished." It's defined by the *Encarta* dictionary as the period
preceding adulthood in *human beings*. An interesting definition,
particularly since the only animals we apply this term to are
humans. There are no "teenage lions" or "adolescent zebras";

only humans have created what playwright Eugene O'Neill once called "Ah, Wilderness." A more empirical definition would mark its beginning at puberty, which is often marked by the beginning of wet dreams for boys and menarche for girls. Puberty is said to end at the age of twenty-one. Neither definition is completely accurate; college attendance can postpone entry into adulthood, and dropping out of school can accelerate maturity. In an effort toward simplification, a friend of mine says that you become an adult when you fill out your own tax forms and no one claims you on theirs. Three things *are* certain, though, about "adolescence": 1) no one knows exactly when it begins, 2) no one knows exactly when it ends, and 3) our understanding of it is determined by shifting social values, e.g., legal drinking age, and political events such as boys' suddenly becoming the "few good men" needed to fight a nation's wars.

Educators mark the beginning of *formalized adolescence* with the onset of the Industrial Revolution, since entry into the labor market by children was considered unethical and eventually unlawful. In no place is adolescence more formalized than in the United States. An entire group of adolescents were renamed "slackers" during the 1990s and evolved into "Millennials" in the early twenty-first century. Adolescence was a way of allowing the youngster to mark time and prepare for the adult world of work. Institutions sprang up that supported this notion, such as high school college-preparatory classes, summer camps, and the Boy Scouts. For middle-class youngsters, the period allowed for working in their fathers' businesses, completing internships, and participating in other creative moneymaking endeavors. For poorer, young working-class people, it was a period of idleness that was broken up by temporary menial work that was virtually disconnected from career planning. Instead, opportunities abounded for adolescents, particularly adolescent boys, to engage in what would be known by the mid-twentieth century as "juvenile delinquency," and the association of crime with adolescence became established and persists to the present day.

But there are groups in which antisocial behavior is not the norm but the exception. Crime, and specifically homicide, among Jewish adolescents is low, as it is for Muslims, Mormons, and fundamentalist Christians—groups that stress service and parochial education. Contrary to media and the repeated utterings of "Baltimore" and "Chicago" by the current occupier of the White House, homicide rates for persons of color have fallen substantially since the early 1970s, narrowing the racial gap. Nonwhite homicide rates, which were ten times higher than those of whites in the early 1970s, are now six to seven times higher. Moreover, the persons who were at greatest risk of being murdered are young adults, representing three-fifths of all victims; males, representing three-quarters of all victims; and American Africans, representing half of all victims. According to the Sentencing Project statistics, it is actually young black males who are far more likely to be murdered than any other segment of the population, though this gruesome statistic has declined significantly since the 1970s.

Homicide rates are highest for young adults in their twenties, but in 2014, the homicide rate for black male teens was forty-six per one hundred thousand, far lower than in the 1970s and 1980s. I believe that much of this decline is attributable to a rising consciousness and social media which have "instructed" young black males on the horrific issue of police violence toward them. It is as if young black males are beginning to fight *against* the stereotypes inaccurately describing them as "superpredators," "throwaway," and useless, and this fight is most evident in the decline in homicidal violence.

Finally, for most adults age forty and older, the risk of being a homicide victim declined over the past two decades. Rates in 2010 are lower than those in 1990 for almost all age, gender, and racial groups. All of this is good news but rarely reported in mass media.

Rites of Passage

Poverty and drug abuse are not necessarily strong predictors of homicidal behavior, even though they appear to be connected. If this were the case, First Nations people would have the highest rate of these behaviors, since alcoholism and poverty are at peak levels in that population. What First Nations people and other groups have in common are traditions and rituals that formally induct their sons into adulthood. These rites of passage occur at various times in the life cycle, and include baptism, conse-cration, weddings, and funerals. All cultures create ceremonies to mark these life transitions with ceremonial rituals, in which families and friends of the initiate participate.

The most visible of these is the bar mitzvah ceremony, when Jewish boys are initiated into manhood at the age of thirteen. The phrase *bar mitzvah* literally translated is "son command-ment," and implies that the boy has a thorough understanding of Jewish law and is formally accepted as a man who participates in the life of the Jewish community. *Adolescence,* while used to describe Jewish boys, is subordinated to the ritual of bar mitzvah. The Jewish *community*—rather than driver's license bureaus, the selective service system, or state legislatures—decides when a boy becomes a man. As with other rites of passage, the ceremony takes place in front of community members to reinforce group cohesion and to pass rituals down from one generation to another.

Rites-of-passage ceremonies in the American African community were disrupted by the period of enslavement. Slowly, the rituals associated with Poro Society were forgotten and replaced by ceremonies taken directly from American culture, which had no relevance to the culture of Africans in the *Maafa na Maangamizi*. Cotillions for girls—still being held among members of what E. Franklin Frazier derisively referred to as the "black bourgeoisie"—imitate what is perceived as being elements of European culture.

Such alienation from African culture is most destructive when it comes to rites-of-passage ceremonies for boys; these rituals define the very essence of what birth, adulthood, marriage, and death mean to the culture. Transition to adulthood is considered the most important passage because it tells the boy what his responsibilities are to himself and to his community. The absence of adolescent rites of passage has made it difficult for black boys to know when they become men. Linking this with the absence of role models, black boys have arbitrarily defined manhood in ways that are often destructive. Fathering babies, carrying a gun, selling drugs, and having sex, while not peculiar to American African culture, are nevertheless viewed by many alienated black youth as appropriate indicators of manhood. While racist media exaggerate much of this macho behavior, it exists in varying degrees among young black males. A young black male once told me that he considered buying a "Glock 26, as opposed to a 19," as being a definite "sign of being a man." I knew what a Glock was, but I was surprised that the fourteen-year-old could distinguish the models. I told him that neither of them made him a man. He asked me what did. I paused and told him the ability to take care of himself and others. He liked that idea, and our conversation ended far better than it had begun.

Rob

Rob, a young black male, wanted to see me because he needed to talk about his explosive anger. I would later find out that even though he was only fifteen years old, he had been physically abusive to two previous girlfriends. I very much wanted to meet this young man, partly because it is very unusual for an adolescent American African male to *ask* for counseling. Stanley Sue's classic study of who uses mental health centers indicates that black males are the least likely to seek mental health treatment, preferring instead to talk with trusted friends or "keep their feelings to themselves."

The next day, at precisely the appointed time, Rob walked into my office, introduced himself, and started asking questions even before he'd sat down. His anxiety was obvious, and he wanted to know what I knew about him. I told him that I knew he had an "anger management problem," and he queried whether that was all I knew. I assured him that it was, and only then did he settle in his seat; his eyes darted around my office as if to absorb anything he could that would expand his understanding of me.

I asked him how he felt, and he immediately responded, "Mad."

"About what?" I asked.

"Everything," he replied.

I asked him if he was angry about coming to see me, and he said no, deliberately leading him into a contradiction of what he just said.

He got the point, smiled, and said, "I guess it ain't *everything*, is it?"

I smiled in return and told him that, like any other emotion, anger can usually be ranked on a scale of one to ten, depending on what is being discussed. As if anticipating my next question, he asked me to name some things, and he would give the degree to which he was angry about them, using my scale, with ten being "extremely."

I said, "Job."

He answered, "Six."

I said, "Girlfriend."

He answered, "Eight."

I said, "Oldest brother."

He answered, "Seven."

I said, "Mother."

He answered, "Twenty."

Wanting to stop there but also wanting to get a broader picture of his rage, I supplied him with a list of words, and his responses clearly showed an enormous amount of fury toward his family, particularly his parents. After a few minutes, I asked him if he noticed a trend, and he replied, somewhat sarcastically, that he didn't need a list to know that and that he could have told me that without my little test. He had become extremely angry, and he ranted about why people ask so many questions and many other things that were only barely related to what we had been discussing. I asked him why he was angry. Stopping short, his mouth still open, he looked at me and said he did not know.

I didn't respond. We both sat there in silence for a few moments until he suddenly burst into tears. I was stunned. Things were happening far quicker than I had imagined they would, and as I handed him a tissue from my desk, I asked him a question that normally would not be asked for many counseling sessions.

"Why do you hate your mother so much?" I asked.

"Because she didn't protect me," he answered immediately.

"Against what?" I queried, disbelieving the speed at which this moment had arrived.

As the ensuing silence engulfed us, I knew that the next words would either be a total lie or an extremely painful truth. Rob said nothing for the next few minutes as he cried softly. I was determined not to break the silence, regardless of how long it took. After a few more moments had passed, he looked up at me and said, "Me being raped in my backyard."

Had I expected this response? No. But had he been a young woman, I might have. I knew that part of my not making the connection was sexist, and I was also surprised at how fast the first session had moved. Only ten minutes into the conference and I had already heard what usually takes days, weeks, or even months to hear.

There is always the possibility that a client is lying. Lying for effect, manipulation, protection, and sometimes for the sheer joy of lying. I also knew that instincts play an important role in counseling, particularly with Cinque's sons. Black men *will* lie to one another as all people lie, but I instinctively knew that Rob was not lying to me. His tears were real, and I knew that his anger and hurt were ready to be expressed and, hopefully, absolved.

I told Rob that what he had just done was probably the bravest thing that anyone could do. His tears were slowing down, and he looked at me, disregarding the pervasive notion that black men should not look each other in the eyes. He said almost disbelievingly, "Really?" and I said yes and explained to him that all pain is real and that the pain he felt had come out in bad ways, but he was brave enough to move into himself and understand where his anger was. He breathed deeply, and unlike so many of my brothers who are waiting to explode and not exhale, he had chosen to deal with his anger at an early enough stage so that it would not consume him when he reached his winter years. Over the next weeks, we talked about anger, frustration, abandonment, rape, lies, fear, goodness, strength, and the many things that Claude Brown's menchildren talk about to very few people. Rob talked about how he was "fairly sure" that his mother knew that his male cousin had raped him, but it was unmentionable to anyone. The sexual abuse was repeated during a three-year period, from the time Rob was eight until he was eleven, whenever there were visits from the twenty-something cousin. His guilt grew out of the fact that he felt he had begun to enjoy the brutal scenes; by the time he was ten, he thought that he was homosexual. His first experience with a girl was at eleven; when he told his cousin about this, the cousin suddenly stopped his molestations. His youthful promiscuity with girls, he believed, was in part due to his trying to bury the memories of his childhood. In all of this, he had kept the ugly secrets to himself, but he felt that his mother's strict attitude toward him was in part due to her blaming *him* for the sexual abuse. The burden of guilt, silence, fear, and anger had taken its toll on the young man, who was unsure about his manhood and where his anger was taking him.

Rob was no different from so many boys whom I have seen over the years, boys who are so confused by their anger that they take it out on whoever happens to be closest. The details of our sessions are not as important as the fact that Rob walked away from them renewed in his commitment to reject the temptations to "be hard" and the avoidance of discussions about the hurt, rage, confusion, and frustration he was feeling. His emotional reconciliation with his family took the form of telling his mother what had happened to him. She had absolutely no knowledge of what had happened to her son. Rob later told me that the tears she shed comforted him, and she told him that she loved him, which provided a bridge to a place where they could meet and learn to love and trust each other again.

Black Rage Revisited

I hesitated in presenting Rob's story at this point because it reinforces the image of "black rage" first discussed by William Grier and Price Cobbs in their 1968 book *Black Rage*. Published during the height of the urban rebellions of the 1960s and on the heels of Malcolm X's assassination, the book seemed the logical explanation for why black people in general, and black men in particular, were so angry. It was supposedly anchored in our inability to express this rage (anger turned inward) safely toward our oppressors. Their dubious psychoanalytic explanations (e.g., how much black women hate their hair, how black people make negative comments about their relatives ["the dozens"]) were quickly grasped by white persons seeking explanations for black anger. Grier and Cobbs were embraced as supporting the long-held notion that blacks were basically "angry" about nearly everything.

White psychiatrists such as Abram Kardiner and Lionel

Ovesey in *Mark of Oppression* and prominent child psychiatrist Erik Erikson, whose racist classification of black identity was immortalized in his most influential book *Childhood and Society,* published nearly seventy years ago, had offered earlier explanations of black anger:

> The babies of our colored countrymen . . . often receive sensual satisfactions which provide them with enough oral and sensory surplus for a lifetime, as clearly betrayed in the way they move, laugh, talk and sing. . . . Three identities are formed: (1) mammy's oral sensual "honey-child"— tender, expressive, rhythmical; (2) the evil identity of the dirty, anal sadistic, phallic-rapist "nigger"; and (3) the clean, anal-compulsive, restrained, friendly, but always sad "white man's Negro."

What is interesting about this strange classification of American Africans is that the book was and perhaps still is a widely accepted treatise for understanding black behavior from a psychoanalytic perspective. It reached its height as a "manual" for understanding black people during the 1960s, when it was carried in the knapsacks of white civil rights workers going south to "help" black people. Erikson was asked to purge this bit of racism in his text in the 1960 revision of the book, but he refused. *Childhood and Society* is now considered a "classic" in the field of developmental psychology.

Where would Rob fit into Erikson's categories? Nowhere. Black anger, though often analyzed, is rarely understood. It is viewed monolithically, with few nuances other than black boys directing their anger toward one another. I believe the obsession with black adolescent anger is an unconscious expression of white anxiety that it may one day be directed toward them. What if black adolescent menchildren today turned their guns from their inner-city brothers toward white suburbanites? What if the anger following the August 2014 murder of Michael Brown decision in Ferguson, Missouri, moved into the white suburbs of St. Louis? Derrick Bell, in his book *Faces at the Bottom of the Well,* talks about how racial themes are developed in America. Black men's lustful attitudes toward white women, the inferiority of black people, and the importance of symbolic gestures toward eliminating racism are a few. Black men killing other black men, a form of self-hate, is also one of them.

What if the "self-hate" turned into simple "hate" and was redirected toward whites? When the late American African psychologist Bobby Wright was asked why blacks kill blacks, he replied that it was because they had not learned to kill whites. A macabre answer, but one that may be the prime motivation for research on black anger. Black men are taught to kill other black men through songs, books, and other people. Charles Silberman, author of *Criminal Violence, Criminal Justice,* expresses the anxiety regarding black anger. It is worth quoting him here at length:

> Blacks are no longer "shy in their acts." The poet Langston Hughes foresaw the change . . . in a bitterly sardonic poem he wrote when the great [black] tenor Roland Hayes was beaten by a white mob in Georgia:
>
> > *Negroes*
> > *Sweet and docile,*
> > *Meek, humble, and kind;*
> > *Beware the day*
> > *They change their mind.*

Wind
In the cotton fields,
Gentle breeze:
Beware the hour
It uproots trees!

The change has come; blacks have changed their minds,
and more than trees are being uprooted. After 350 years
of fearing whites, black Americans have discovered that
the fear runs the other way, that whites are intimidated by
their very presence; it would be hard to overestimate what
an extraordinarily liberating force this discovery is. The
taboo against expression of anti-white anger is breaking
down, and 350 years of festering hatred has come spilling
out. [Italics added]

When it comes to black adolescents in their autumn years, their understanding of this fear is virtually nonexistent. Most adolescent black males do not understand how much whites fear blacks, and they get in trouble because of this. Jim Myers, in his book *Afraid of the Dark: What Whites and Blacks Need to Know About Each Other,* opines that popular wisdom among American Africans says that blacks must understand how whites fear them and compensate for this:

Whites are so often unsure of themselves that blacks recognize they must approach the situation in ways that will put whites more at ease. In fact, there is a large body of conventional wisdom in black America about how to deal with white people in ways that will not stir white fears. For example, it is said that you always have to tell white people what they want to hear; that it's not wise to let them know you have strong opinions or are knowledgeable about anything; or you must never let white people suspect they're not smart or in total control of the situation.

Black boys will eventually learn this, as do most blacks, and to the degree they do, they will navigate white institutions more or less easily. During the autumn years of black boys' lives, Young Warrior Councils must teach them this without compromising their integrity. Understanding white institutions is important, but the lesson should never come at the expense of personal integrity. "Selling out" is often a misused term among young brothers when applied to young black men who deal effectively with majority institutions. It *can* be used to describe black men who give unquestioning loyalty to systems that hurt them and their people.

White fear is expressed in many ways, such as the incredible police presence gathered to "keep the peace" when nearly two million black men gathered in Washington in October 1995. Hollywood is the best purveyor of this white fear of black anger. In *48 Hours*, Eddie Murphy's first film, there is the line, "I am your worst nightmare—a black man with a gun."

Black Adolescent Health

Health in adolescence is largely determined by the quality of health care received during childhood. Frequency of immunization, for example, varies significantly by race. The following figure shows that blacks and Latinos have the lowest immunization rates when compared to whites and Asians. Easily controlled

CHART 8: RECEIPT OF RECOMMENDED VACCINATIONS*
AMONG CHILDREN AGED 19–35 MONTHS, BY RACE/
ETHNICITY,† 2013

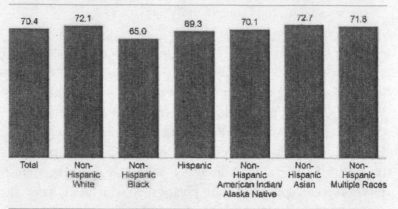

70.4	72.1	65.0	69.3	70.1	72.7	71.8
Total	Non-Hispanic White	Non-Hispanic Black	Hispanic	Non-Hispanic American Indian/ Alaska Native	Non-Hispanic Asian	Non-Hispanic Multiple Races

*Recommended Full Series: ≥4 DTaP, ≥3 Polio, ≥1 MMR, 3 (4) Hib, ≥3 HepB, ≥1 Varicella, ≥4 PCV.
†Estimates for Native Hawaiian/other Pacific Islander children were not available.

Source: U.S. Department of Health and Human Services, Centers for Disease Control and Prevention, National Immunization Survey. Retrieved from: http://www.cdc.gov/vaccines/imz-managers/coverage/nis/child/data/tables-2013.html. Accessed September 4, 2014.

diseases such as rubella and pertussis become problems as black boys enter their autumn years. Linked with inconsistent health care at early ages are the myths concerning violence among black males. Drugs and alcohol are usually involved with violent crime, and the widely held perception is that adolescent black males use these substances as psychological "oil" in order to commit the crimes. In fact, drugs are used at nearly the same rate by blacks and whites primarily in the commitment of crime, as shown in Chart 9. When it comes to alcohol use in criminal acts, whites far exceed those of black offenders.

The drugged-out, hulking, gun-toting black adolescent in a dark hood and baggy pants and looking for violence is a myth.

The fact remains, however, that black boys in the autumn

CHART 9: DRUG OR ALCOHOL USE BY OFFENDER

Race of Victim	Total	Alcohol	Drugs
White	100%	34%	9%
Black	100%	26%	11%
Asian	100%	27%	8%

Source: Bureau of Justice Statistics, *American Indians and Crime*, February 2004.

of their lives die faster and more frequently than other boys. I believe this is due, in part, to the absence of rites-of-passage ceremonies for black boys. The Native American vision quest, the Jewish bar mitzvah, and even adolescent baptism in more fundamental Christian churches are all rites of passages that celebrate a boy's journey into manhood; as such, these ceremonies have a major impact on them. Roland Gilbert and Cheo Taylor's *Simba*—Kiswahili for "lion"—program, which was established during the 1990s, has provided rites-of-passage ceremonies to dozens of boys in California. According to Taylor, they have had a profound change on the boys and their community: "Violence, crime, poverty, drug abuse and murder can be totally eliminated by people making different choices. These choices are made as a result of how individuals see themselves and others, and how they think, feel and act towards themselves and others."

Autumn Warrior Councils

While throughout their lives black boys are at risk for having health problems, being victims of homicide, and being under-taught by schools, their teenage years are, paradoxically, a

time of danger and a time of opportunity. There is an obsession among social scientists for detailing the challenges of black
male adolescents while providing few remedies for overcoming
these problems. Of course, they have a high rate of fratricide;
of course, their educational issues need elaboration; we already
know most of this. This is a critical period for black boys; it is the
stage when options for changing self-destructive behavior are
fewer and paths to social extinction wider. The Young Warrior
Councils need to be even more vigilant in making sure these
years are successfully negotiated.

The Warrior Councils should prepare for a rites-of-passage
week when Young Warriors reach the age of thirteen; this ceremony should be attended by the council members who have
been involved with the boys for thirteen years. The oldest member of the Warriors Council should direct the rite-of-passage
ceremony. That young black men understand how elder black
men have dealt with racism and other obstacles in their lives is
important; therefore, the ceremony should include a one-hour
video interview with an elder male in the community who is at
least seventy years old.

At the end of the week, the boy conducting the interview
should present the video to the council. During this same week,
the *elder* should interview the *initiate*. These two interviews
serve a dual purpose: to gather information and to bond the
boy to his past and his future. The elder black male becomes
a true "role model" for the boy and teaches him his obligations
to the American African community. A study done by Dr. Raymond Coward of the National Institute on Aging revealed that
older blacks are twice as likely to receive total care by family
members than older whites. By listening to their elders recite
"how they got over," young boys need to understand that "care"

is more than medical care. The interviews also give the elder an opportunity to reconnect with his past, renew his sense of self-esteem, and continue his contributions to the future of his community.

Rites-of-passage ceremonies vary greatly from city to city and community to community, similar to the way Poro Societies vary in West Africa. I have participated in a variety of these ceremonies around the country, and I am excited by the creativity of those involved. The type of ceremony is not as important as the encouragement to Cinque's sons to continue a tradition that began centuries ago but was all but lost during the period of enslavement. That the ceremonies incorporate the same African-centered values found in the ancestral homeland of black Americans is important. Rites-of-passage ceremonies provide social support for American African males, much like the psychological and social support that helped them survive the *Amistad* and free themselves to return home. All rites-of-passage ceremonies should contain the following:

1. Two rites-of-passage ceremonies should be conducted during the year for the seven Young Warriors. For boys born between January 1 and June 30, a ceremony should be conducted on or before July 1. For the Young Warriors whose birthdays fall between July 1 and December 31, a second ceremony should be conducted on the first night of Kwanzaa (*Umoja*). Invitations for the two ceremonies should go to members of the boys' immediate family, other relatives, and friends.

2. The oldest man and oldest woman in the Young Warrior Council should perform the pouring of libations. The libation ceremony should honor the boy's thirteen-year involvement

with both the Birthing Circle and the Warriors Council, and should honor the ancestors and link the young man with his ancestral ties to Africa. For example, the elders could pour water on a plant in front of the gathering. A sample libation recitation that can be shared by the elder man and woman during this part of the ritual follows:

> Ancestors, we know that you are honored by [name of Young Warrior] being here today. [Pour part of the water into the plant.] He has been with us for thirteen years, and honored the sacrifices that all of you made while you were on earth. [Pour more of the water into the plant.] [Name of Young Warrior] has the spirit of Malcolm X, the patience of Joseph Cinque, the strength of Martin Delaney, and the kindness of his father [substitute names as appropriate for the boy, and pour a third portion of the water]. We know that you will be with [name of Young Warrior] as he begins his journey into manhood. We know that he will be strong, wise, and kind to his family, to women, to children, to other brothers, and to himself. [Pour remaining water.]

Libation recitation can take many forms, but keeping the boy and the ancestors central to the ceremony should be paramount.

3. The boy's immediate family should make three brief testimonies. This can be done by the parents, guardians, and/or siblings of the boy and should take no more than ten minutes.

The testimonies should praise the boy, recite humorous anecdotes, and provide proof to the gathering that the boy has been mature and deserves to be called a man.

4. An elder woman should then read a passage (no more than five minutes) from a black writer that has been meaningful to the boy during his life. The elder woman should explain why she chose the passage, then read the text that is symbolic of the initiate's life.

5. Similar to the previous reading, the boy should read a passage that is meaningful to him. It, too, should be no more than ten minutes and carefully chosen.

6. Following this, the gathering should watch the video interview. It should be shown without comment; if done well, it will convey the importance of older black men mentoring younger ones. A brief discussion should follow, with the initiate and the elder man answering questions from the audience.

7. As the final act of the ceremony, the same elder man and woman who opened the ceremony should give to the boys a larger piece of *Kente* cloth. This should be followed with gifts to the new man and a *karamu,* in which all participate.

Remember, this is a *suggested* rites-of-passage ceremony. It is provided as an example; the creativity of the Young Warrior Council can embrace a variety of rituals conducive to inducting the boys into manhood. After the ceremony is complete, it is paramount that the councils continue their once-per-month meetings and maintain support for the boys as they enter full adulthood.

How should this be done? Like Poro Society, if the Warrior Council has been taught correctly, the young men will have a set of values based on the Four Cs. They will have a broad understanding of their obligation to family, community, and themselves that will equip them, as Cinque was equipped, to cope with an assortment of social, legal, and educational circumstances. But the Warrior Councils must reinforce these values until the young man is twenty-one. Initially, this should occur in the monthly meetings, but gradually, over a period of two years, the young men themselves must continue their association with one another, much as Cinque relied on the Mende men captured on the *Amistad* to secure freedom for all fifty-two captives. According to court documents and eyewitness accounts, the Poro Society that the Mende captives of the *Amistad* belonged to persisted during their Connecticut imprisonment. They consulted with and made suggestions to one another, appointed Cinque as their primary spokesperson, and passed along to one another information that would shed light on their captivity. The Warrior Council should promote comparable conduct among the new initiates. Members of the council will find that the Young Warriors naturally appoint leaders among themselves for certain tasks and responsibilities. The young men should never be encouraged to model themselves after "Black Greek letter" fraternities that often haze their new members and have values only tangentially related to African-centered values.

The cohesiveness among the Young Warriors will be severely tested if one of them "gets into trouble." Trouble can occur if one of them is arrested or detained for things he did not do. The legal preparation they received during their summer years will be tested during such periods. The adults in the council should have names of attorneys, physicians, and other persons readily available when legal crises arise. The council should act on behalf of the young man for events that he is too young to handle. At all times each member of the council should carry the phone numbers of all the other members so that they can reach one another quickly. This is very important; adolescent black boys are often coerced into confessions by law enforcement agents. On several occasions, I have seen young black men sitting in parking lots, and on curbs, handcuffed, with several police cars surrounding them. Officers yelling and headlights glaring in their faces make for a horrendous scene, with the terrified youngsters looking bewildered and afraid. While I am sure that the heavy-handed tactics used by police can sometimes be justified, I am equally sure that in many cases they are not. Police brutality and harsh sentencing are real and are directed disproportionately toward young black males. Young Warrior Councils should be aware of such data and do whatever they can to help their members avoid contact with the criminal justice system, as well as help those who do come in contact with law enforcement.

Educational Issues

The investment club should have grown substantially by now, with an eye toward ensuring that each of the seven Young Warriors is looking toward education beyond high school. Time should be set aside in the regular monthly meetings to discuss both current and future educational issues affecting the boys' lives. Continued exposure to black male role models should

reinforce the idea that formal education is of paramount importance to Young Warriors.

During the eleventh grade, tours of historically black colleges and universities should be planned, and the testing and
application procedure should be guided by an adult member
of the council. The boys should schedule time with their high
school guidance counselors; council members must monitor
these sessions since black boys' aspirations are often detoured
in these offices. I have asked dozens of *teachers* about their own
"guidance" during this period, and many have reported hearing discouraging words from insensitive counselors about higher
education. At Morgan State, students have reported to me how
white counselors discouraged them from attending a historically
black university in favor of a local community college. Counselors may ask disparaging questions about the "quality" of education students may receive, despite the fact that historically black
universities have produced W. E. B. Du Bois, Nikki Giovanni,
Martin Luther King, Toni Morrison, and so many more. The
councils should act as a watchdog over such bad advice and, as
during the other seasons, intervene if necessary.

Work

All Young Warriors should be encouraged to work after school
when they turn sixteen. Part-time work outside the home
teaches discipline and increases children's economic responsibility. A portion of the Young Warriors' pay should be set aside
for the investment fund. However, working outside the home
should never interfere with the boys' education. In this sense,
all extracurricular activities, including work, should be subju-

gated to the boy doing well in middle and high school. The boys should integrate the principle of *Ujima* (collective work and responsibility) into how they conduct themselves in whatever work they do. Work should be valued as a learning experience, even if it involves flipping hamburgers or ushering at a sporting event. Elders should teach how the value of work is linked to the community and how money can contribute to uplifting persons within it. Respecting places where people work is also important. When I was a child, my mother once told me that we should be careful about littering in public buildings because "nine times out of ten, one of ours is cleaning it up at night." This axiom stuck with me throughout my life, and it was an early lesson in respecting the work of others.

Black Men and Women

At each stage, the Young Warrior Councils discuss the primacy of the relationship between black men and women. All of the rituals involved in bringing the boy to manhood show the importance of black males learning to respect black females. Poro Society consistently taught its initiates the importance of respecting women and deemphasized sexist attitudes toward girls and women. The autumn Warrior Councils should focus some of their activities on frank and open discussions about sexuality and its role in the healthy development of black couples. In particular, council members should invite counselors and physicians to join discussion groups. Often adolescents distort information about sex regardless of race. Autumn may be the last time this information is shaped in a positive way for the boys. Warrior Councils should conduct lengthy discussions on the history of black male and female relationships during this period. Familial relationships among Africans in America were damaged by enslavement's legacy, and still linger despite denials by White Way parents. Randall Robinson's book *The Debt: What America Owes to Blacks* shows how white privilege's bitter fruits were nurtured by the roots of slavery sunk deep into the barren soil of American racism. He makes the all-too-often-ignored connections between contemporary American institutions and their embarrassing connections to slavery. Aetna Life, the largest life insurance company in America, for example, insured the lives of slaves from its beginnings in 1853. Slave owners took out policies on their slaves and received death benefits when they died. Nothing, of course, was given to the deceased's immediate family. In 2000, Aetna "apologized" for this history and its CEO referred to it as a "deplorable practice." Young Warriors during their autumn years should learn this history; those who encourage people to "forget about it and move on" should be viewed with suspicion. The subject of reparations for the Western enslavement of Africans should be thoroughly studied by the Warriors; studies should include lectures and guest speakers fully versed in the subject.

Since the success of Terry McMillan's *Waiting to Exhale*, young people have read a spate of black romance novels with the fairly common theme of almost irreconcilable problems between black men and black women. Even before these books, Michele Wallace's 1979 bestseller, *Black Macho and the Myth of the Superwoman*, was dubiously touted by *Ms.* magazine as one of the most important treatises ever written by a black woman. In *Black Macho*, Wallace analyzes from a feminist perspective the sexual dynamic of the transition from civil rights to black liberation. This is what she found: "There is a profound distrust, even hatred between black men and black women. It has been nursed along not only by racism on the part of whites but also by an almost deliberate ignorance on the part of blacks about the sexual politics of their experience in this country."

Hatred between black men and black women? In some cases, yes. But in most cases, no. Persons who couldn't care less about our relationships often do focus on the problems between black men and black women. White feminists proclaimed *Black Macho* to be a frank discussion about the relationships between blacks, as if such a discussion were really important to the white feminist movement.

Moreover, films and books during the 1980s created heated discussions on this incendiary topic. *The Women of Brewster Place* and *The Color Purple* were both met with ridicule and scorn by insecure black men who saw Gloria Naylor and Alice Walker as "betrayers of black manhood." In fact, these books and films merely scratched the surface of deeper problems that have existed for centuries between black men and black women under white supremacy. These books drew attention to the inherent sexism during the civil rights period when freedom for American Africans was somehow associated with men and not women. "Prone," the infamous answer by a civil rights worker about where the best "place" for women was during the 1960s, had been challenged by Ella Baker and other women. They found new energy with Angela Davis, Alice Walker, and bell hooks, who gave renewed meaning to Sojourner Truth's words that "among the blacks there are women and among the women there are blacks."

But rarely were substantive dialogues between black men

and black women held regarding the wedges that had been deliberately driven between them by racism. More radical theorists, such as Haki Madhubuti and Neely Fuller, saw this as the essential problem between us. However, it is tempting to focus on the more obvious results of racism's *impact* on these relationships than on the actual *source*. After all, conservatives say "white supremacy" is a slippery, vague, and nebulous concept, similar to Melville's great white whale. They argue rather weakly that it remains elusive and becomes even more so when it is attached to contemporary relationships between black men and black women.

It was easy to see how such disruptions occurred during our period of enslavement, with the rape of black women, their sale by the masters, and the controlled sexual access that black women and black men had with one another on plantations. It is much harder to see how, 160 years later, the residual effects of slavery would haunt our relationships, even though Toni Morrison writes about it in *Beloved,* and Alice Walker in *The Color Purple.* Black men and black women, through the ingenious nexus of Hollywood and the media, would eventually blame each other for the difficulties between them, leaving racism out of these discussions. It is worth repeating Ayi Kwei Armah's view, in his book *Two Thousand Seasons*, of how our relationships were the focus of white supremacy:

> *There is no beauty but in relationships.*
> *Nothing cut off by itself is beautiful.*
> *Never can things in destructive relationships be beautiful.*
> *All beauty is in the creative purpose of our relationships;*
> *All ugliness is in the destructive aims of the destroyers'*
> *arrangements.*

Armah believes, as do I, that the primary attack, which dislo-
cated black men and black women from Africa and one another,
was deliberate and was expressed in many ways. The inability
of black men and black women to protect one another during
enslavement produced feelings of impotence and helplessness
on both sides. Neither could protect their children from being
slaughtered, beaten, or sold. The reality behind the poignant
portrayal of Kizzy being sold in *Roots* was the greatest threat to
the parents of any enslaved child. The last narratives spoken by
enslaved American Africans during the 1930s on their enslavement indicated a morbid fear of being sold that was often used
to coerce them into subjection.

Nothing changed during the Jim Crow era, when nearly
every day black men and black women were lynched some-
where in the United States. Accounts of these lynchings hor-
rify the readers and question the humanity of the perpetrators.
James C. Cobb cites a case recorded in the *Vicksburg Evening-
Post* during the 1920s in which a black Mississippi couple was
lynched for allegedly killing a white man:

> The blacks were forced to hold out their hands while one
> finger at a time was chopped off. The fingers were distrib-
> uted as souvenirs. The ears of the murders [*sic*] were cut
> off. Hobert was beaten severely, his skull was fractured,
> and one of his eyes, knocked with a stick, hung by a shred
> from the socket. . . . [A] large corkscrew . . . was bored
> into the man and woman . . . and then pulled out, the
> spirals tearing out big pieces of raw, quivering flesh. Then
> the crowd burned them at the stake, after partially filling
> their mouths and nostrils with mud to prevent a fast death
> from smoke inhalation.

The lynching of Mary Turner, reported in *The Crisis* in 1918, confirms the inability of black men and black women to protect one another from violence. After her husband had been lynched in Valdosta, Georgia, Turner made the mistake of making public her intention of seeing her husband's murderers put to death. When word of her defiant promise reached those who had participated in her husband's murder, they kidnapped her from her house. Although she was eight months pregnant, she was hanged upside down from a tree and bathed with gasoline. After burning her clothes from her body, her stomach was cut open and the infant fell to the ground. It gave out a whimper before a man crushed the baby's head with his shoe. When found, Ms. Turner's body was riddled with hundreds of bullets. Her murder was casually reported by the press as the result of her "unwise remarks" concerning her husband's death.

Throughout the civil rights era the violence directed toward black men and black women continued with the notorious killing of Emmett Till, the arrest of Rosa Parks, the beating of Fannie Lou Hamer, and the assassination of Martin Luther King Jr., to name only a few. We often forget how both men and women were affected by this violence. Emmett Till's mother told the Chicago funeral directors to leave her son's coffin open so that people could see the horrors done to her son. In 1955, she had sent her son to Money, Mississippi, to visit relatives; the fourteen-year-old Till on a dare flirted with a white female store clerk named Carolyn Bryant. A few days later, Bryant's husband, Roy, and J. W. Milam abducted Till from his uncle's house. His body was found three days later, beaten beyond recognition, an eye gouged out, and a bullet in his skull, which had apparently been crushed with an ax. Till was found in the Tallahatchie

River, weighed down with a 150-pound cotton-gin fan. Blacks were terrified, and it was simply unthinkable for one to testify against a white man accused of a racial crime. However, Emmett's sixty-four-year-old uncle, Mose Wright, defied custom; at risk to his life, he agreed to be a witness at the trial of the two men accused of killing Emmett. When the prosecutor asked Wright to identify the men who had abducted his nephew, he stood up, pointed to Milam and Bryant, and said, "Dar he."

In the end, however, Wright's incredible courage made no difference. Milam and Bryant's attorney told the all-white, all-male jury in his closing statement, "Your fathers will turn over in their graves if [they are found guilty], and I'm sure that every last Anglo-Saxon one of you has the courage to free these men in the face of that [outside] pressure." The jurors listened to him, deliberated for about an hour, then returned a "not guilty" verdict. The foreman later said, "I feel the state failed to prove the identity of the body." I remember as a child being afraid to go to sleep after looking at the gruesome photo of Till displayed on the cover of *Jet* magazine.

In our mind's eye, we also see the famous funeral photo of Coretta Scott King and her children, and we realize the enormous impact that racism has on the relationships of black men and black women. The women in James Byrd Jr.'s life suffered after his lynching in Jasper, Texas. His decapitated body, after being dragged by three white men on a lonely Texas road, was the crime he paid for being a black man at the wrong place at the wrong time. Dr. Thomas Brown, the pathologist who testified at Byrd's murderers' trial in 1999, described the victim's last moments in his testimony, which was quoted by the Associated Press and Reuters:

Brown said the 49-year-old Byrd was still alive as he
bounced down the road June 7, breaking most of his ribs,
shredding his knees and his elbows, fracturing bone and
tearing cartilage. Brown said Byrd struggled with his torso
to keep his head off the road, and in the process was castrated.

The pathologist said Byrd was probably conscious until
he grew so weary that his body flipped off the road and
into a concrete culvert, about halfway through his three-
mile ordeal, when his "head, shoulder and right arm were
separated."

Prosecutor Pat Hardy described those last moments:
"The gentleman was alive and was alive up until the time
he pretty much exploded when he hit the culvert. And you
can imagine the pain he went through from the injuries
he had."

His aunts, sisters, and mother shared in the horror of his
death at the hands of murderous white males, who have in the
past haunted and continue to haunt our relationships. We often
forget how the horrors of racism affect black men *and* black
women, and mediate our relationships in a variety of ways.

This is a sordid but necessary history for Young Warriors to
learn during the autumn of their lives. Taught correctly, these
stories will instill within them a sense of how they can either
contribute to this history or teach others how the sacred bond
between black men and black women should be preserved.
Elders in the councils should teach that it is not by accident
that images presented to young black people are part of a long
history of destroying the sacred bonds between black men and
women stolen from Africa.

Conclusion

Despite the role of discipline in the autumn Warrior Councils, these groups should not be viewed as militaristic or rigid. Monitoring young men's progress does not mean that there is no room to attend sporting activities, proms, field trips, and other activities of a typical teenage boy. The councils play a stabilizing role in the boys' lives and become an extended family that they can rely on. Each boy is simply surrounded by a true "village" that helps him learn what being a man is all about. The autumn years are important for this lesson; it is the last period when the boy is dependent on adult supervision. These lessons need to be learned well as the young man enters the winter of his life.

8

The Seasons of Our Sons: Winter, Ages Twenty-two Through Homegoing

For you are father to the orphan, husband to the widow, brother to the rejected woman, apron to the motherless. —KHUN ANUP, 1650 B.C.

Harold

His oldest son was in jail, and he had just suffered his second heart attack. Bills were left unopened on the kitchen table because there was no money to pay them. His two youngest sons were in school and needed financial support. His pride eventually yielded but prevented him for many years to allow his wife to work; he adhered to the strictest of Eurocentric beliefs that only he could be the "breadwinner." His two daughters were out on their own, the oldest married to a southern man who loved her dearly, the younger one in and out of an abusive relationship with a man who would eventually die of a heart attack before reaching forty.

Since this was during the pre-bypass era, it was impossible to do anything about Harold's heart. It beat as best it could and was fed nitroglycerin when it didn't do that very well. Shredded wheat, skim milk, and other healthy foods had nearly replaced the unhealthy diet that he, like most American African men, indulged in. Harold tried hard to stick to the healthy regime so that he might eke out a few more beats and thus a few more years with his family.

I saw him during this period angry, abusive toward his wife, sullen about having to work so hard, and depressed because he was uninsurable due to his heart condition. When Harold purchased his first house at the age of fifty-one, it was more stimulating, at least psychologically, than the defibrillator that had been used to restart his heart on several occasions. He also bought his first car a year later—a Deuce and a Quarter—that was as long as the living room in the new bungalow that meant so much to him and Dorothy. They began to travel widely, to places like Pittsburgh, Toronto, and Chicago, in the silver-and-black Buick. He helped his oldest son find a good job despite his prison record. Even though Harold had not gone to college, he was adamant that his two younger sons would, and he helped them to do so with both emotional and financial support. He dispensed wisdom that would stay with his children long after he'd gone from their lives. "If you make your bed hard, you've got to lie on it" and "He who knows and knows he knows is wise; follow him" were two of his favorite quotes.

Like most older black men—older being any who survive the age of fifty—Harold was focused on making sure that there would be a legacy to pass on to his children and his grandchildren. He knew the mistake he had made in waiting to buy a house, treating his wife violently, and simply working too hard when he should have taken it easy. During Thanksgiving gatherings, Christmas celebrations, and family reunions, he began to teach his children from his own experiences. He would speak to them, usually one-on-one, as if he did not want to risk the possibility that someone would challenge him. His sons and daughters would relate what he said privately to one another and swap the information among themselves. They had forgiven him of his past wrongs and were understanding of things that were happening to him physically and emotionally at this time in his life.

At sixty-four Harold died of a stroke as he sat waiting to take Dorothy to work. As he quietly hummed to himself, a blood vessel popped in his head; he breathed his last breath, then slumped over in his favorite chair. Dorothy walked into the living room, saw him in the chair, and began to cry. She would follow him with lung cancer just four years later, and my brother Ron and I would choose the spot in the cemetery where they would rest together with the ancestors.

Like so many other black men, my father knew that life was lived in a world of white supremacy. He railed against it from as far back as I could remember, and he always told us to do the same. It was frustrating to see how the white world punished him for standing up against discrimination in the steel mills of Pittsburgh and the unions of Cleveland.

He had been living in Pittsburgh when Josh Gibson played with the Homestead Grays in the Negro Baseball Leagues, and he was an avid baseball fan. He bragged about the fact that Babe Ruth, that American icon, couldn't hold a candle to Josh Gibson's power at home plate. I realize now that baseball was to black men during the Depression what basketball is for young black men today. They lived it, talked about it, and were proud of Jackie Robinson's resilience against racism. Dad was a good ballplayer in his own right, and he taught his sons the game, as well as how to keep meticulous box scores for all of the players, especially the 1950s black players, such as Larry Doby and Minnie Minoso.

He knew that he had often treated my mother badly, and he tried to make up for it as he grew older. Part of the obligation of being a black man during his winter months is to tell others what they need to know about navigating the waters of racism in school, work, and social situations. My father did this as best he could with the tools he had, while supporting his family during a period when doing all of this was very hard. His children saw this and understood it.

We Are the Men Our Ancestors Prayed For

My father resisted. Sometimes he was successful, sometimes he wasn't. Our generation of black men no longer has to succumb to physical and psychological control the way our ancestors had to during their enslavement. We have choices. To be sure, these choices still occur with a backdrop of racism, but we have them and can exercise them effectively when we factor in how racism mediates these choices. We can enter the courts to seek redress for wrongs against us. Like Cinque, we can let people know that even though they view us as only recent members of the human race, we come from a long line of strong men, and will continue to be so for centuries to come. We always understood the importance of letting others know we had brains; we just didn't have the wherewithal to show it. So even though we know our sons have only a 1 in 52,000 chance of being a player in the National Basketball Association, we still encourage playing the sport for the sense of teamwork and dedication it inspires.

We can no longer act as conduits for drugs in our communities or sell our souls to Hollywood studios and record company executives, just for meager monetary gain and the sanction to demean our brothers and sisters. We fail at capitalizing on our popularity like Ronald Reagan, G. Gordon Liddy, Oliver North, and Bill Bradley, and so we are left wondering what a Michael Jordan, or Kareem Abdul-Jabbar might do as a senator or president. We agonize to a man when we see our brothers shooting each other, and we rejoice with them as a Mandela and a Tutu tell the world what time it is.

Winter starts at twenty-two in the lives of black men. This is a dangerous time for us, the period when we direct the greatest homicidal violence toward one another. The only way to counter or prevent this violence is early intervention—Birthing Circles, Young Warrior Councils, the Four Cs—which will heighten self-esteem, self-awareness, and, subsequently, lower the number of homicidal deaths among young black men.

Role Models

Black men, for they are now indeed men, should begin to tell their peers what being a man means to them. Black boys who become men and shun drugs, violence, and predatory behavior toward their community should all be viewed as role models rather than those who have finished college, or have become "successful" businessmen. *Role model* is a much misunderstood term and has become increasingly meaningless when used in terms of aiding the American African community to achieve certain goals. A noble concept, it is oversold as a way to help black boys in trouble. In many cases the idea is a way of opting out of doing the hard and necessary interventions that would truly change the boys' lives for the better.

Like other black professional men, I have been asked on numerous occasions to be a "role model" for young black boys and girls by doing volunteer work and by simply being around them. My ambivalence about this designation lies in my feelings not so much that such volunteer work is useless, but that it limits the definition of "role model" to black professional men.

Recently I was asked to participate in such a session honoring a "leader" of a midsize city in the South. He was rich, powerful, drove a luxury car, and lived in an all-white neighborhood. Based on these acquisitions, he was considered "successful." I had little respect for the brother, who was being touted as a "role model," because he had done numerous things to harm black people in the city. He smiled as he received the award, and I thought about the numerous people he had professionally assassinated at the behest of his white benefactors. He now epitomized the notion of a Super Slave as his white sponsors told the wide-eyed boys sitting before him how he was a "role model" for them. In older times he would be considered a "credit to his race"—now he was simply a puppet of color for whites, and was used as a disruptive force in the local American African community.

It is difficult for black men to sanction men like these publicly since it bruises egos and creates divisions within our communities. In 1998, Randall Robinson publicly criticized Vernon Jordan, bringing scathing rebukes by several black journalists who saw Jordan as a power broker who deserved respect and deference. Critiques of American African communities by so-called neoconservatives are often applauded and blessed by whites. Publicly denouncing our "role models" as sellouts to the needs of all black people is dismissed as the ravings of marginalized radicals. I have watched such nationally known black "leaders" in various arenas proclaim their disdain for Louis Farrakhan, to the overwhelming praise of their powerful white benefactors. Black men must be careful that the role models they become are not mere cardboard caricatures of white persons who ultimately do not want the best for American Africans. Furthermore, they must measure the worth of any leader by deeds, not words, and they must choose carefully whom they repudiate or praise so as not to be manipulated by whites who feel threatened by independent black men and the power they wield.

What Can Black Men and Women Learn About Each Other?

American Africans are taught to eat generously from the bounties of white supremacist culture but only nibble at knowledge about themselves. The old saying in American African communities that the "white man's ice is colder than the black man's" reflects another rumor of inferiority that somehow "theirs" is better than "ours."

It is the same with black men's and black women's knowledge of one another. I have given workshops on black relationships in which I ask how many black men and black women there are in the United States. The range of answers has not to do so much with educational levels or cultural intelligence as it does with the lack of accurate information about black men and black women beyond popular media. There are simply too few books available for us to know hard-core facts about each other. We often enter heated discussions about our relationships based more on fiction than fact. The appalling lack of hard information shared between us determines many of the ways we interact with one another, and creates misunderstandings and faulty generalizations about what we mean to each other.

One piece of information that enlightens our relationships is the *sex ratio,* which is defined as the number of men per one hundred women in a selected population. When just these data are presented to workshops of black men and black women, a lightbulb seems to go on in the room. Chart 10 illustrates the sex ratio since 1920 for whites and blacks in the United States, the implications of which are enormous. Slightly over 1.8 million black women in the United States have no men of marriageable age available for them. These figures do not include black men who are gay, confirmed bachelors, in relationships with non-

CHART 10: UNITED STATES SEX RATIO BY RACE: 1920–2010

Year	Whites	Blacks
1920	104.4	99.2
1930	102.9	97.0
1940	101.2	95.0
1950	99.0	93.7
1960	97.4	93.3
1970	95.3	90.8
1980	94.8	89.6
1990	95.9	89.8
2000	96.3	90.1
2010	95.1	86.6

Source: U.S. Census Bureau.

black women, or incarcerated. Adding these to the total number of "unavailable" black men could increase the figure to 2.5 million. This discussion should not be construed to imply that black women *need* a black man in their lives. Indeed, there are black women who are lesbian, single by choice, committed to white men, or in prison. What is important is that black women have fewer choices than their white counterparts when it comes to the availability of men.

Many books and magazines feature articles about these numbers. Some black men even take perverse advantage of it. Often black women get angry about it. I have heard black women say, "Men are a luxury" and "I don't need a man in my life." This may or may not be true, and in some cases Cinque's sons reinforce these ideas by their actions toward women. I have heard black men brag about the fact that their choices of women are vast because they are "in demand." My megalomaniacal brothers who say such things have no anchoring in African traditions that seek balance rather than power in their male-female relationships. They are psychologically immature when it comes to conducting healthy relationships with women, and they see women as things to be manipulated rather than persons to be cherished.

The bitterness that many black women feel toward black men in many cases is well founded. Brothers can do better but often don't. They rationalize their misogyny in rap lyrics that degrade black women. Claiming that this is what "the sisters want to hear" and referring to women as female dogs strengthens the alienation between them. Moreover, viewing a black woman as "a bitch" puts her even lower than the "dawg" black men "affectionately" call one another.

At a recent speaking engagement at a historically black college, several young black men just entering the winter years of their lives defended their use of the terms *bitch, dawg,* and *nigga,* despite very vocal protestations from the women in the audience. The men were firm in their belief that these terms were endearing and showed affection for themselves and "their women." Only a handful of black men in the audience objected to their use, and these men were derided for being "punks." One woman in the audience looked pleadingly at me and said that this is why there are so many problems between black men and black women—because we are not listening to each other. Her words rang true, and I asked her what could be done to improve the communication. She said that we simply don't listen to one another, that we already have our minds made up about where the other is coming from. I agreed.

Toward the end of the second decade of the twenty-first century, there is little listening and even less communicating between black men and black women. Perhaps the sheer gap in numbers forces us to talk about and not listen to one another. One female told me during a Kwanzaa celebration, "Sisters don't have enough black men to 'practice' on in the most basic interactions." I asked her what she meant, and she said that black women have to imagine what black men feel, think, and do because there simply aren't enough to demonstrate what being a black man is all about. She went on and compared learning about black men with learning to swim: you can read all the books in the world about it, but you really won't learn anything unless you jump in the water. Her metaphor ended with her comment that there was no pool, no water, and no bathing suits for many women who simply want to know things about black men. "We are left to guess what black men want, feel, think, and know, and we simply have no place to practice these things."

One place to practice these things is social media and dating sites, but they should not take the place of real world interaction. In the age of the Internet, illusion is often the software of modern-day non-relationships. Illusion creates cyberspace relationships that are often based on who we aren't. Images, strokes from a keyboard, texting, email, and Skype, are one- and two-dimensional ways of "knowing" a person. These devices can *supplement* but never replace genuine face-to-face interaction. It is the African way to experience the goodness and messiness of a person, in three and four dimensions. By touching, talking, laughing, smiling, frowning, seeing a small momentary glance, twinkling of an eye, or hearing the craziness of a thought, we know who that person is and possibly who they will be in our lives.

A deliberate psychological education must begin if black men and black women are to get to know one another. A few years ago a female friend and I began running groups called Seminars on American African Relationships (SOAR), in which for two hours once a week black men and black women simply talked to one another about themselves and the things important to them. The fifteen to twenty members, half men and half women, expressed their delight in meeting and just talking. After a month, however, we noticed that a few black men were beginning to fall by the wayside. I called several of them, and they reported that some of the things being said in the group were hitting "too close to home" and that they were feeling uncomfortable. I encouraged them to come back and talk to the group about their experience, though I knew it wasn't going to happen. Not wanting the group to become disproportionate by gender, I told the remaining members how the brothers felt. Surprisingly, both men and women said that these were simply excuses for miscommunication or for no communication. They believed that

the men who left would leave anyway and opt for "safer" com-
munications, which in their case meant no communication at all.
The remaining members wanted to continue, despite the three-
to-one ratio that had resulted from members dropping out. I was
not sure that the group should dismiss the men who'd stopped
coming so easily. Should they be coaxed into returning to share
their feelings? I think that black men are taught at young ages to
hide, suppress, and otherwise ignore the part of them that may
be considered tender. One might argue that this has nothing to
do with color, since all men are emotionally inhibited. All men
are, but black men have inherited a social climate where speaking one's thoughts can actually be dangerous. My father, similar
to other black fathers, taught us what to say when confronted by
white police officers. We were also taught how to talk to white
bosses and how to avoid making white males feel threatened by
our presence. Most white males receive a surplus of confidence
builders in social situations since their environments affirm their
white maleness. Not so with black men. The machismo taught
to black boys beginning at early ages sometimes works to keep
them insulated against racism, but it discourages expressions of
love, hurt, and pain. It leaves black women feeling alone in conversations with us; the communication is often a one-way effort,
met on occasion with a grunt from black men. In group situations with other black men, bullshitting replaces true expressions of feelings. If a brother does gather the courage to speak
of his vulnerability with another black man, he can be faced with
ridicule or dismissed as a punk.

I have observed black filmgoers, both male and female, laugh
at black films such as *Beloved, The Hurricane,* and *American
Gangster* that are emotionally painful to watch. The laughter is
a defense against seeing our own condition placed on the wide

screen and being unable to connect with the helpless feelings that are uncovered. Black men are particularly prone to dismissing feelings that make them less "hard" in a world that requires hardness for survival.

Black boys, who often hear the older women in their lives make negative comments about black men, are subject to this early push toward emotional isolation. The lover who ran out on her, the father she never saw, the brother who is unwilling or unable to help financially—are all bogeymen projected onto her impressionable young son. Black men must be bad because Mom says they are bad, the boy reasons; without contrary evidence, these phrases become mantras boys repeat to themselves and other black boys. They grow up with ideas about manhood that are heavily influenced by women who may be bitter about men. Joined by some brothers who are simply trifling, young black males become the tangible results of self-fulfilling prophecies. This vicious cycle will continue unless very early intervention takes place.

Healthy Black Relationships: Beloved in Our Lives

The inability of black men and black women to sustain relationships unmediated by race has been nearly total since they were first captured in Africa. This topic, if discussed, would create greater cohesiveness in our relationships. Morrison's ghostly child-woman Beloved, in her book by the same name, represents how the relationships between black men and women are haunted by the unresolved racism that has damaged them.

Sethe's poignant words about her rapists, "They took my milk," are still relevant to what black women face today. They should discuss this connection with the men in their lives. Likewise, black men feel a connection with Halle, whose insanity was triggered by watching the rape of his wife and being unable to stop it. It is important for black men in the winter of their lives to share this connection they feel with their women. To suppose that Beloved's ghost no longer haunts the lives of black people in America, and indeed the world, is delusional. She is the fruit of the horrors we sustain as we try to establish families for our children and ourselves. The chokeberry tree on Sethe's back, kissed by Paul D, is a reminder of how black men and women should seek to heal the wounds inflicted on us by a culture determined to sever bonds between us.

Black men in search of the woman who will be "the one" in their lives should take heed of Sixo, Paul D's friend at Sweet Home, who walked twenty-eight miles once a week to be with his "Thirty-Mile Woman" for one hour. His description of what he wants in a woman is one of the most sublime in black literature:

> Paul D sits down in the rocking chair, and examines the quilt patched in carnival colors. His hands are limp between his knees. There are too many things to feel about this woman. His head hurts. Suddenly he remembers Sixo trying to describe what he felt about the Thirty-Mile Woman. "She is a friend of my mind. She gathers me, man. The pieces I am, she gathers them and give them back to me in all the right order. It's good, you know, when you got a woman who is a friend of your mind."

"A friend of your mind." Morrison's words are as important to women as they are to men. I have seen in my work black women who knowingly opt for men and women who are not friends of their mind. They do not effect the healing described in *Beloved*; instead they are wandering hopelessly in relationships that are meaningless, attributable to black men being "just dogs" and black women who are "just bitches." This is a simple conclusion to a problem that we rarely discuss among ourselves at functional levels. A female friend of mine once told me that she would never discuss her problems with white people or with black men. Moreover, she told me that many of her black female friends were simply dysfunctional when it came to black male/female relationships. My friend was living with a lot of pain, confusion, and anger, but she has no communication with black men who are the source of much of her anger. Ultimately, these situations all too often translate into negative comments made about black men in front of black boys in the spring and summer months of their lives. They hear too often that black men "ain't shit," and they begin to harbor the anger that eventually translates into the poisonous hate-filled lyrics of unconscious rappers paid handsomely by record executives to ignite further misogynistic behavior among black boys and men. It is a vicious cycle.

In the end, Beloved disappears, after Sethe confronts her demons and the black women of Cincinnati provide her with spiritual support for her unresolved pain. What is important, however, is that her exorcism is incomplete until Paul D returns to her life and tells her, "You your best thing." Sethe is unbelieving until he answers her question, "Me? Me?" Only when he answers yes can they begin their long journey to reconciliation and understanding. It is the same for us today.

9

A Summary of the Seasons

Historians have speculated for years about the *Amistad* incident and its leader, Sengbeh Pieh. Few people in American African history have had the impact on the treatment of Africans in America more than Pieh. What motivated him to rebel against his enslavement and direct his captors to take him back to his homeland of Sierra Leone? How could he effect such a successful rebellion with a handful of men and women on a voyage that his buyers saw as a relatively routine "shopping trip" to purchase Africans to work on their sugar plantation in Cuba? The answer to these questions can be found in Pieh's Poro Society training and the fact that his captors took for granted that they had effectively crushed any thought of rebellion out of the enslaved Africans. His early training in Sierra Leone afforded him an advantage over those who had captured him. He had been schooled in understanding the world around him, including the importance of knowing the laws and customs of other peoples. His captors, on the other hand, assumed that the gru-

eling journey from Africa aboard the *Iesora,* and the seasoning
that took place in Cuba, would have broken his will enough that
he would submit to whatever they meted out to him. They were
hoping for strong but passive "slaves" when they purchased the
Africans in June 1839, and they dismissed the possibility that
the Africans could *rethink* their enslavement and escape to
freedom.

It is the same way today. Black boys can be raised to have
a remarkable sense of who they are and what their place is in
the world. They can be educated to understand what the world
expects of them and how they can change the negative opinions
held by educators, law enforcement officials, and policy makers;
they can create effective strategies for change in their communities. A summary of these strategies is outlined below:

I. Child–Rearing Strategies of Black Parents

Method	Description	Strategy	Results
White Way	Traditional way of raising black boys. Parallels the way of raising white boys.	Sees institutions as impartial in their delivery of services to black boys. Attempts to get black boys to adjust to the system.	Children run into conflict with institution. Parents or teachers see them as troublemakers and encourage system submission.

Method	Description	Strategy	Results
Gray Way	Challenges institutions regarding treatment of black boys.	Views institutions objectively and is willing to advocate on behalf of black boys. Heavy involvement with institutions through which black boys pass. Willingness to challenge bureaucracies. Organizes other parents and teachers.	Experiences conflict with bureaucracies. Children and adults feel more empowered regarding their ability to change systems.
Black Way	Sees systems as inherently out of touch with black boys' life goals.	While protest is part of strategy, it is a means to an end. Teaches African-centered principles to boys.	Creation of institutions that are responsive to needs of children. Healthy black boys.

II. The Ten Commitments to Raising Black Boys

1. Maintain a strong commitment to educating black boys.
2. Possess a deep and abiding knowledge of global black history.
3. Read at least thirty minutes a day on African/African American culture and life.
4. Be comfortable in predominantly black environments.
5. Attend African-centered religious institutions.
6. Volunteer at least five hours a month in human service activity that engages black boys.
7. Understand all bureaucracies that impact black boys.
8. Organize against environments oppressive of black boys.
9. Read the following five books:

    Beloved by Toni Morrison
    Yurugu by Marimba Ani
    The Miseducation of the Negro by Carter G. Woodson
    There Is a River by Vincent Harding
    The Art of War by Sun Tzu

10. Teach at least two other persons each month about the Ten Commitments.

III. The "Four Cs" for Raising Black Boys

Consciousness:

• Begin at young ages to read out loud to boys about heroes and sheroes among American Africans.

• Insist that school systems recognize various cultural holidays that are relevant to Africans in the *Maafa na Maangamizi*.

• Provide a broad listening repertoire to black boys that includes jazz, reggae, rhythm and blues, gospel, funk, symphonic works by black composers, rap, and soul.

• Take opportunities to visit museums, library exhibits, and other community activities that present black history.

• Encourage black houses of worship to supplement your boy's education by having at least three hours of classes per week devoted to the study of black history.

• Provide educational films that teach the history of Africa, the period of enslavement, and its aftermath.

• Expand images beyond the famine, war, and disaster that characterize coverage of the continent by news organizations.

• Encourage the wearing of African clothing at young ages.

Commitment:

• Be willing to intervene on behalf of black boys at any level to enhance their life chances.

• Make volunteering with black boys for five hours a month an initiation rite for all members of black social organizations.

Cooperation:

• Establish more "Mother's Day/Evening Out" programs at American African churches so that single parents can get relief from parenting.

• Encourage adoption among black houses of worship.

• Create reading groups sponsored by black male civic and religious groups that support black boys' reading about African American culture and life.

Community:

• Use Title VI of the 1964 Civil Rights Act to ensure the equitable distribution of federal dollars for local projects.

• Monitor and attend school board meetings in school districts.

• Create political action committees (PACs) that serve the special interests of the black community.

• Target for selective buying businesses that have a history of harassing and underemploying American Africans, particularly boys.

• Systematically write congressional representatives to make sure they are responsive to legislation that affects the lives of black children.

• Create booster clubs that encourage the purchase of computer technology for black children.

• Organize groups of American African houses of worship to build educational facilities to meet the needs of black children.

• Encourage black houses of worship to create credit unions for the communities they serve.

• Where possible, place money in American African–owned banks.

• Sponsor summer-abroad study programs in Africa.

IV. Birthing Circles

▶ Designating a person to monitor the mother's prenatal care, i.e., making sure that appointments are kept and accompanying her to doctor visits during the pregnancy

▶ Designating a person (male or female) to join the mother for prenatal Lamaze, nutrition, or exercise classes

▶ Designating a person to serve as a backup for completing the paperwork associated with childbirth

▶ Designating a person to serve as an information specialist on such things as naming, postbirth ceremonies, and health information

▶ Designating a person to accompany the mother into the delivery room

V. Young Warrior Councils

The fifth year should include the following activities:

▶ Members of the Young Warrior Council and the seven Young Warriors should hold monthly meetings.

▶ Each of the seven Young Warriors should read three age-appropriate books during the first year.

▶ The newly formed Young Warrior Council should take field trips, discuss healthy living, and provide science instruction and lectures that teach the boys about African history and culture.

▶ At the end of twelve months, the Young Warrior Council should conduct an agreed-upon ceremony that inducts the boys into their sixth year.

▶ The sixth year should repeat the basic curriculum of the fifth year, adding information technology as a key component of the learning process.

▶ The seventh year begins the study of law and media.

▶ The seventh and eighth years should expand on what the Young Warriors have already learned, particularly in the areas of media and law.

▶ The ninth and tenth years are critical in the development of Young Warriors, and the councils should be very vigilant in monitoring the institutions that are instructing their boys.

▶ The eleventh and twelfth years are looking-ahead years for the rites-of-passage ceremony, celebrating the seven Warriors turning thirteen.

These checklists summarize the central methods for raising healthy black boys in America. They should be adapted to the needs of the local communities in which they will be implemented, and serve as guidelines for the persons in charge of the Young Warrior Council.

10
Epilogue

Parable of the White Elephant

All American Africans and well-meaning nonblack people in
America should be outraged at what has happened and continues to happen to black boys and men in this country. When they
hear about Tamir Rice, Michael Brown, and Philando Castile,
the high incarceration rates of black males, drugs and the CIA
connection, low levels of academic performance by young black
males, and so on, there should be a cry for retribution and
change from those who claim to want the best for black boys
and men.

Instead, what is found is a free-floating frustration toward black males by people tired of hearing their "excuses." Books, articles, and television programs woefully lament the "vanishing black family" abandoned by the black male who has been proclaimed, like some animal, to be "an endangered species." Many black women discuss the shortage of "good" black men and wistfully talk of the importance of being "flexible" in securing companionship, which often means going beyond traditionally constructed racial and gender boundaries. Rarely do any of these "analyses" factor in racism/white supremacy as related ostensibly to nearly every condition facing black people. Racism and its not-so-subtle perpetrators, such as conservative radio talk-show hosts and presidents, have been extraordinarily successful in making it unpopular to attribute anything negative associated with black males to skin color. Explanations in these directions are cast as an attempt to "play the race card." Discrimination's mutable presence has lulled black males and others into thinking that whatever happens to them is completely their fault and that they need to "quit blaming the white man" for their fate.

Imagine you own a family compound you built from the ground up. It is neat, clean, well ventilated, and has all the accoutrements that you need to live. Your extended family lives in the compound, and you enjoy their presence each day when you return from work. Cooperative management of the compound based on ancient values makes it an Eden-like place.

One day you come home to find a large white elephant wreaking havoc inside the compound. It is trampling over everything you built, defecating on the walkways, uprooting the elaborate shrubbery that took years to plant and prune, destroying everything in sight.

You straighten things out as best you can, but the elephant continues its rampage. It ignores your pleas to leave. In fact, it attempts to trample you. You continue to repair, clean, and rebuild the home, but the white elephant continues to come periodically, hell-bent on its mission of destruction. You organize your relatives to ward off the beast, but the elephant continues to destroy, despite your collective efforts to fend it off. Debates ensue within the family about the best way to destroy the animal; it has killed members of the family that the compound was designed to nurture and protect.

A decision is made by desperate family members to ignore the beast and instead focus on the animal's destruction. Eventually, you devote all of your energy to cleaning up and replacing the things the animal has destroyed.

You actually begin to ignore the elephant and adjust to its destructive behavior. Family members continue to be lost, but little attention is devoted to understanding the wild elephant. All of your energy is focused on cleaning and repairing the damage wrought by the beast. You encourage your family members to do the same.

Other compounds in the neighborhood have had similar visits by white elephants, and you tell your friends to ignore them, to focus instead on the damage the elephants cause.

Eventually, you die, but your message has penetrated the minds of your descendants: they believe the white elephant, still on a rampage after many years, is only a secondary problem, and so they, too, focus on cleaning materials, wood, bricks, and mortar, to try to rebuild after the rampaging white beast metes out its destruction. An entire culture and literature evolves around repairing furniture, building more sturdy walls, painting and redecorating, while the elephant continues to destroy. The elephant itself is all but forgotten by members of your family and the neighboring compounds.

Like the white elephant, racism's influence on everyday behavior among both blacks and whites has become so acceptable that we rarely even see the beast, though it may stand directly in front of us. Members of the black community may advise that we ignore the white elephant, and may actually blame its victims for the destruction in their lives. Racism is so inherent and accepted that even talking about it as a primary reason for explaining the conditions of American African males is ridiculed. "The post-racial era," though wished for, is not practiced. Cinque's sons are still left without a father to guide them, theories to understand them, and institutions to support them.

Though Joseph Cinque returned to Africa, he never really went home. His two years in captivity had taken a toll on his village and family. Speculations to this day abound over what happened to him. Some say he went to Jamaica (rumors persist that he is buried there) and began to dabble in the same slavery that had taken him from his family. This gossip, provided mostly by members of the American Missionary Association, whose officials were miffed at Cinque's rejection of Christianity after they had been instrumental in his defense, attempted to discredit him and to reinforce the notion that you could take the "heathen" out of the "jungle" but that the "jungle" would remain within the "heathen."

Other rumors had him staying in Sierra Leone, only to die at the doorsteps of the AMA after a long illness. His great-grandson Samuel Hingha Pieh, who has blessed me with his prologue to *The Warrior Method*, believes this is the most likely scenario because it fits with eyewitness reports of his rebuilding his life as much as he could in his native Mende land. Though he never found his wife or his two daughters, he was reunited with his son, Kolima. They worked together in Christian missionary work until Sengbeh's death in 1879.

I have always wondered what happened to Sengbeh Pieh's immediate children. Surely, they wept at their father's captivity. What did they think as they watched their mother beaten and their father dragged off on that dusty Mende road? What did she tell them once the dust had settled? Did they go after their father? Were they captured also? If they were, did they go to Jamaica or Brazil? Did they die a peaceful death in Sierra Leone? Did his grandchildren immigrate to America, and if they did, from what country? Are his descendants in New York? Sao Paulo? Kingston? Chicago? Los Angeles? London? Perhaps they were brought to America and lived just a few hundred miles from where their father was captured and eventually tried.

The period of enslavement continues to bring confusion and paradoxes to Africans in America and throughout the *Maafa na Maangamizi*. Cinque's children's children's children could be in school with your son or daughter. They might work next to you. They may be in a managerial suite at a Fortune 500 company, or they may be victims of the drug culture financed by the Central Intelligence Agency during the 1980s in Los Angeles. Cinque's sons are found in the faces of all black men who took the nails from the *Amistad* and made them keys to their freedom.

In November 2014, Tamir Rice a just-turned-twelve-year-old boy was playing with a toy gun on the playground in my hometown of Cleveland, Ohio. Two police officers, Timothy Loehmann and Frank Garmback, responded to a 911 call that "a male" was pointing a pistol at people and that Tamir was most likely a juvenile and that the pistol was "fake." In less than two seconds after exiting their police car, Officer Loehmann (fearing for his life) shot twice and killed young Tamir.

I am angry when I know that the lives of my black children and men are only a thread's width away from a similar fate. I am more concerned now than I was yesterday about white police who stop me, and I still reminisce about the criticism I received years ago that I was "too overprotective" of my son when he wanted to take his girlfriend out on a date. Tamir is dead, but his killer walks free; this sends the not-so-subtle message that a black man's life means little. Why do blacks have to convince America that the lives of black men are just as valuable as those of white men? Why do we accept it as so? As Ella Baker put it, "We who believe in freedom will not rest until the killing of black men, black mothers' sons, is as important as the killing of white men, white mothers' sons."

Perhaps Cinque would not be so surprised about how his own captivity and humiliation are reenacted in the everyday harassment of black men who drive, walk, and breathe while being black. Like Cinque, they can all too quickly become captives of a legal system that makes being a black man suspect. Police harass black boys at play and at work much the way they did during enslavement, when black boys were watched, manacled, carded, and pulled over by white men who were anxious about their presence.

Cinque's sons are a metaphor for black men today. Too many of us have been exiled in America for such a long time that our black souls have only a partial understanding of our origins. When our ancestors were forced through the "doors of no return" on the west coast of Africa, never to see their homeland again, much was retained, but more was lost. Our skills as blacksmiths, farmers, bankers, musicians, artists, and physicians honed in various Poro Societies were retained. We used our skills during our enslavement to build the economies of the

Western world. What was eventually lost was the history of the various people crammed aboard the slave ships that scattered us throughout the world. So many black men have lost the sense of who we *were* that today it is difficult for us to know who we *are*. The gap between what we know now and what we were in West Africa can be closed by *going back* through the "doors of no return" psychologically, culturally, and, in some cases, physically to rediscover what was left in our ancestral homeland. There is nothing radical about this. White Americans do it when they encourage the presidents of the United States to reconnect with their Irish ancestry. Mexican Americans do it with Cinco de Mayo festivals. The Irish Americans do it with St. Patrick's Day. Passover revisits the spiritual and cultural roots of Judaism. Reconnecting with one's ancestral roots is not only common among American ethnic groups, it is institutionalized in various celebrations and holidays.

On several trips to Africa, I have been overcome with emotion in the dungeons at the Castles of Ghana, part of the stone structures that dot the west coast of Africa that held millions of my African ancestors captive as they waited to be shipped like cargo around the world. A systematic and deliberate psychological and physical torture was practiced on the captives in an attempt to poison their positive images of Africa. But Africa persists in the music, art, science, and bodies of black people captured on the shores of West Africa. It is felt in street drumming, seen in Savion Glover's tap dancing, heard in the lyrics of Kendrick Lamar's raps, seen in Denzel Washington's acting, tasted in Carver's peanut butter, translated in Coltrane's music, and admired in LeBron James's moves to the hoop.

Black men in America have their ancestral roots on a continent so very far removed from the consciousness of the vast majority of black males in the *Maafa na Maangamizi*. This is not accidental. The removal of African culture from the minds of Africa was systematic and took place over centuries; it continues with the negative images of the continent portrayed by the media. I know that far too many African minds in America are distorted by European values that so permeate their lives that it seems difficult to see what good West African values can do for us today. Images of Africa are emblazoned on media that show swollen bellies, floods, famine, and war. If only Kosovo, Northern Ireland, and Chechnya were shown on CNN, revulsion toward Europe would match that which has been created after centuries of negative portrayals of Africa. Black boys in America are increasingly estranged from their African roots and are given names that reflect this alienation because they teach us nothing about ourselves. Italian names such as Antonio, English names such as William, and French names like Leroy are but one small indication of how far from Africa black boys begin their lives. Commonly absent as they grow from childhood to adulthood are the Four Cs—consciousness, commitment, cooperation, and community—the essential ingredients for their survival in a society that encourages their destruction.

Like other holding stations on the west coast of Africa, the Castles of Ghana in Elmina and Cape Coast contain openings known as the "doors of no return," the final exit to the ships where black bodies were stacked for transport to various parts of the imperialized white world. Parents, educators, and others who wish to raise, teach, and understand black boys in America must go from ship to shore through these doors to Africa, both physically and psychologically. Like the mythical *Sankofa* bird of Ghana, whose head is tucked under its wing and looks backward, they must return to a mind-set when black men knew who they were, what their place was in the world, and what expectations were put upon them. It will be a difficult journey, but it must be made if Cinque's sons are to survive in America. Enough studies have been made, conferences held, and theories offered about the "problem" of black boys in America. It is time to reopen the "doors of no return" to discover what was left in Africa, and shape it to fit the needs of black boys for their past, present, and future.

Acknowledgments

I have been humbled by the global impact *The Warrior Method* has had. A couple of years ago, I was on a crowded commuter train traveling to the twentieth anniversary of the Million Man March and a young brother, recognizing me, whipped out a copy from his backpack. It was well-worn, with yellow stickies coming out on all sides, and another reminder of how ubiquitous the book has become. Since its 2001 publication, it has affected the lives of thousands and brought me into contact with people I would have otherwise never met. I've been privileged to give workshops about the method in Ghana, Tanzania, Trinidad, London, Sydney, Nova Scotia, Jamaica, Saint Kitts and Nevis, and throughout the United States and many other places too numerous to name here. Warrior Circles now exist all over the world, and while I used to keep track of them, it is now impossible to do so. Not a month passes that I don't receive an email, phone call, text, or letter from mothers, fathers, boys, the incarcerated, educators, and politicians about how the book had touched their lives.

The first book did not anticipate the dawn of social media nor a black president, and the updated version discusses both of these subjects and how they affect our images of black boys and men.

Writing a nonfiction book about black boys poses challenges at several levels. Convincing publishers that black boys are important and have their own voice, editors that black boys have a story to tell, and a public that is largely afraid of black boys to listen to them are not easy tasks. I want to thank Amistad for recognizing that their voices are very important, especially in light of the public executions of black boys that took place during the past ten years and throughout American history. I want to especially thank Tracy Sherrod, editorial director for Amistad HarperCollins, and Amber Oliver for their help in making this book possible.

The Warrior Method could not have been possible without the gentle hand of Carol Taylor guiding it to completion. The ancient and sacred balance between black men and black women is expressed perfectly in the book. She not only was an extraordinarily gifted editor for the original book, but understands what being African in America is all about.

The late Manie Barron of Amistad was my final editor who taught me a lot about the politics of the publishing industry. He was a solid brother who was willing to take chances with black authors. May he rest in power with the Ancestors.

Morgan State University has been supportive in allowing me to have the time to write as well. Its generous role in providing its faculty and students with many opportunities to examine black life is a tradition I am proud to be a part of.

No author writes in a vacuum. The persons who've most influenced my way of thinking are the late Frances Cress Welsing, Neely Fuller, Marimba Ani, Derrick Bell, Malcolm X, Ida B. Wells-Barnett, and W. E. B. Du Bois. I share their African-centered worldviews and hopefully have done them justice in talking about race, racism, and black males.

Fisk's eminent librarian Jessie Carney Smith; Yaa Asantewa Nzingha, a true African-centered educator; my uncle and aunt Herbert and Ardella Campbell; Jennifer Williams gave me much-needed spiritual advice; Harry Allen of Public Enemy, whose analysis of victimization is nothing short of brilliant; Tiki Mercury-Clarke for providing much-needed help with Kiswahili; my late brother Ron who made his transition since the original book was published and his son, Nick, and his wife, Jasmine, and daughter, Nicole; Anne and Pat, the mothers of my children; daughter, Sharifa; my two sons Omari and Faraji; spirit son Jawanza; Samuel Pieh, great-grandson of Sengbeh Pieh; my dear friend Cynthia Mason; Archbishop Emeritus Desmond Tutu and his daughter Nontombi; Adar Ayira for her insight into how oppression works; Jerry Laster for being a faithful friend for fifty-plus years; Jeff Menzise, my friend and colleague at Morgan State; my five grandchildren, Jason, Jordan, Samarria, Aubrielle, and Taylor, all are both direct and indirect influences for the ideas in *The Warrior Method*.

Finally, my mother and father, Dorothy and Harold Winbush, always taught their sons and daughters to "tell the truth no matter what the price." I wish I could say that I've done that all of the time, but I haven't. This book, however, reflects the truth-telling honesty they encouraged in their children, Harold Jr., Myrna, LaVonne, Raymond, and Ronald. Ultimately, the challenges faced by black boys are challenges faced by all black people. The unpopular truths contained in these pages will be rejected, consciously or unconsciously, by those persons who dismiss the continuing influence of racism in America, and accepted by those who, regardless of color, wish to confront the problems faced by black people in this country.

Ray Winbush
Baltimore, Maryland, May 2018

Annotated Bibliography

Ani, Marimba (1994). *Yurugu: An African-Centered Critique of European Cultural Thought and Behavior.* Trenton, NJ: Africa World Press.

The most comprehensive African-centered critique of European systems of thought ever written. The extraordinary breadth of Ani's book provides a starting point for understanding how various European philosophies undergird white supremacist systems. One hundred years from now, this book will be cited, along with Du Bois's *Souls of Black Folk* and Ralph Ellison's *Invisible Man,* as one of the great works that analyze the condition of Africans throughout the diaspora.

Armah, Ayi Kwei (1979). *Two Thousand Seasons.* Chicago: Third World Press.

The question is constantly asked: "Why are Africans in the shape they are in?" Armah provides a disturbing answer through a searing novel. He forces the reader to examine the complicity of white supremacy in the condition of African people.

Asante, Molefi (1988). *Afrocentricity.* Trenton, NJ: Africa World Press.

A book that describes what is now accepted as one of the most important worldviews of the twentieth century.

Asante, Molefi (1993). *Malcolm X as Cultural Hero and Other Afrocentric Essays*. Trenton, NJ: Africa World Press.

Asante gets specific about issues confronting Africans in the diaspora ranging from the image of Malcolm X to violence among Africans.

Asante, Molefi and Abu S. Abarry (eds.) (1996). *African Intellectual Heritage*. Philadelphia: Temple University Press.

If you need one book that provides the vast intellectual scope of African people it is this one. Beginning at 2150 BCE and ending with the Million Man March, Asante and Abarry present the readings and speeches of African people. A fundamental book for any library involving African people.

Asante, Molefi and Mark Mattson (1991). *Historical and Cultural Atlas of African Americans*. New York: Macmillan Publishing Co.

This book provides a panoramic view of the history of African Americans—from Egypt to the present. Asante provides a wealth of photographs, drawings, and maps that help to locate African people geographically, historically, and psychologically. An essential book for understanding African people.

Barboza, Steven (1993). *American Jihad: Islam After Malcolm X.* New York: Doubleday.

Barboza explores the varieties of the fastest growing religion in America. His interviews with Muslims from all walks of life provide an unprecedented view of Islam.

Bell, Derrick (1992). *Faces at the Bottom of the Well: The Permanence of Racism*. Basic Books.

A life-changing book. The former Harvard professor provides a grim scenario on why African Americans will never achieve "equality" in this country. A pessimistic yet very realistic book about racism.

Bernal, Martin (1987, 1991, 2006). *Black Athena, Vols. I, II, III.* New Brunswick, NJ: Rutgers University Press.

The sheer audacity of Bernal's thesis—that what we call "Greek civilization" is essentially Egyptian—makes these volumes "heavy" reading. The scholarship is unquestionable in Bernal's pursuit of the true root of what is commonly called "Western civilization."

Bowen, W. G. and Derek Bok (1998). *The Shape of the River.* Princeton, NJ: Princeton University Press.

The former presidents of Princeton and Harvard Universities provide the most compelling arguments on why affirmative action works. It destroys myths such as it displaces whites or is "a handout," by giving the reader empirical evidence of its positive results. A must-read for anyone who wishes to avoid the hype on affirmative action.

Bradley, Michael (1978). *The Iceman Inheritance.* New York: Kayode Publications Ltd.

Bradley offers the controversial thesis that European racism is evolutionary and biological. Bradley supports this theory with numerous references and forces the reader to examine the possible origins of white supremacy.

Brooks, Roy L. (ed.) (1999). *When Sorry Isn't Enough.* New York: New York University Press.

The issue of reparations for Africans will dominate any racial dialogue during the first quarter of the twenty-first century. Brooks's book provides a context for these upcoming dialogues by making a strong case that the nonpayment of reparations represents a continuing crime against humanity toward Africans and their descendants.

Butler, Octavia (1995, 2003). *Parable of the Sower* and *Parable of the Talents.* Aspect and Seven Stories Press, respectively.

The African grande dame of science fiction, Octavia Butler, pens two novels that are prophetic in nature about the current deterioration of the United States and the "West" in general. Butler paints a grim picture of California beginning in 2025 that is eerily familiar to contemporary events in the world today. Mesmerizing in their narrative, these two books that should be read in order make for lively discussions on how Africans should be mindful of survival in a dying world.

Butterfield, Fox (1996). *All God's Children: The Bosket Family and the American Tradition of Violence.* New York: Harper Perennial.

No other book links the current violence in the African community with the American tradition of violence better than Butterfield's. Willie Bosket, one of the most violent criminals in the United States, is a direct product of the history of mayhem, torture, and "the duel mentality" that is traced back to before the American Revolutionary War. The analysis is compelling and answers many of the questions about how the United States is the most violent nation in world history.

Chideya, Farai (1995). *Don't Believe the Hype: Fighting Cultural Misinformation About African-Americans.* New York: Penguin Books.

The sheer volume of misinformation about African Americans is a primary contributor to "rumors of inferiority." Chideya's small but very informative volume presents an array of facts that may surprise even those who think they know dearly held "truths" about African Americans. A useful handbook for combating racist stereotypes.

Comaroff, Jean and John (1991). *Of Revelation and Revolution: Christianity, Colonialism, and Consciousness in South Africa.* Chicago: University of Chicago Press.

Presents the argument as to how Western Christianity was the fundamental rationale for the establishment of apartheid in South Africa.

DeGruy, Joy (2005). *Post Traumatic Slave Syndrome: America's Legacy of Enduring Injury and Healing.* Milwaukie, OR: Uptone Press.

The legacy of enslavement has left a deep wound in the psyche of African Americans that many will deny, some will acknowledge, and few understand. DeGruy, who coined the phrase "Post Traumatic Slave Syndrome," effortlessly shows the direct links and residual effects of enslavement on *all* African Americans. A powerful book that must be read, especially by educators and human service workers.

Diop, Cheikh Anta (1974). *The African Origin of Civilization.* Westport, CT: Lawrence Hill Publishers.
The African genius who first cited anthropological evidence that the Egyptians were black people. A scholarly book that will change your view of Africa.

Du Bois, W. E. B. (1903). *The Souls of Black Folk.* Available in a variety of editions through a variety of publishers.
"The problem of the twentieth century will be the problem of the color line." Du Bois's prophetic words echo even louder as we near the end of the century where color is still unresolved as a problem. If you have not read this book, you have no foundation for understanding anything relative to Africans in America.

Du Bois, W. E. B. (1896). *The Suppression of the African Slave Trade.* Available in a variety of editions through a variety of publishers.
The best book to understand how the United States circumvented its own abolition of the slave trade in 1808. Du Bois argues that this was primarily for economic reasons, i.e., the expansion of the United States as an industrial nation. This was Du Bois's doctoral dissertation at Harvard and written when he was only twenty-eight years old.

Du Bois, W. E. B. (1946). *The World and Africa.* Available in a variety of editions through a variety of publishers.
Written as a rebuttal to European historians who said that Africa did not contribute anything to "civilization," this book shows the reader that not only were such assertions incorrect, but they were grounded in white supremacist notions about European superiority and African inferiority. A get-acquainted volume to the importance of Africa in understanding the world.

Franklin, John Hope (1989). *Race and History: Selected Essays, 1938–1988.* Baton Rouge: Louisiana State University Press.

A collection of the most important essays by one of America's leading historians. The sheer sweep of his writing opens new vistas on the struggle of African Americans, and excites the reader to further research.

Fuller, Neely (2016). *The United Independent Compensatory Code/ System/Concept: A Compensatory Counter-Racist Code, Revised Edition*. Washington, DC: NJF Productions.

Read by anyone who wishes to truly understand the nature of white supremacy and its global impact on persons of color from around the world. Neely Fuller's self-published book, available at black bookstores around the country, has been a bestseller for years among those who wish to deconstruct the subtleties of white supremacy. Must-read.

Gould, Stephen (1981). *The Mismeasure of Man*. New York: W. W. Norton.

Gould analyzes the rampant nineteenth-century white supremacy that plagued all of the social and natural sciences. Essential reading if one is involved in the natural sciences.

Griaule, Marcel and Germaine Dieterlen (1986). *The Pale Fox*. Chino Valley, AZ: The Continuum Foundation.

The classic French anthropological study of the Dogon people of Mali provides a context for understanding indigenous West African religion. The study leaves no doubt about the harmony between science and religion in the Dogon cosmology.

Grimshaw, Anna (ed.) (1992). *The C. L. R. James Reader*. London: Blackwell Press.

Some have called the late C. L. R. James the "Socrates" of Africans in the diaspora. This would probably be an insult to James, since most consider him far wiser than the Greek with whom he is compared.

Harding, Sandra (ed.) (1993). *The "Racial" Economy of Science: Toward a Democratic Future*. Bloomington, IN: Indiana University Press.

Critics of Afrocentricity argue that the "natural" sciences are immune to criticisms of racism and androcentricity. Harding's selection of readings proves that if anything, the "natural" sciences are deeply imbued with racist ideology that advocates the exploitation of first-world persons.

Harding, Vincent (1983). *There Is a River: The Black Struggle for Freedom in America.* New York: Vintage Books.

Simply the best history of Africans in America ever written. Harding takes the reader from Africa to the Civil War from the point of view of being African in America. A work of sheer beauty.

Holloway, Joseph E. (ed.) (1990). *Africanisms in American Culture.* Bloomington, IN: Indiana University Press.

This book examines the sometimes unnoticed influence that African culture had on the development of American linguistic formation, games, holidays, and food.

Holloway, Joseph E. and Winifred K. Vass (1993). *The African Heritage of American English.* Bloomington, IN: Indiana University Press.

Holloway and Vass give remarkable examples of the debt owed to the linguistic contributions of Africans in America. Place-names as well as maps are provided to show how influential Africans were in naming many locations throughout the United States.

James, Marlon (2009). *The Book of Night Women.* New York: Oneworld Publications.

"Slave narratives" are always difficult to read, but James's depiction of life on a Jamaican plantation during the 1800s ranks as one of the best depictions of the cruelty and barbarity of Western chattel enslavement. His characters are very complex and the women in the book rank as some of the most memorable in fiction. Simply one of the best narratives of the ironies and inhumane cruelties of the worst crime against humanity of the past millennium—the transatlantic slave trade.

Karenga, Maulana (1993). *Introduction to Black Studies*. Los Angeles: Kawaida Publications.

No other book presents as much information in so few pages as Karenga's book. The creator of Kwanzaa, this book provides a basic outline on how black studies should be approached.

Lewis, David Levering (1993). *W. E. B. Du Bois: Biography of a Race*. New York: Henry Holt and Co.

Du Bois's life, spanning nearly a century, is the story of blacks in the twentieth century. His genius and commitment to fighting racism is brilliantly detailed by the author. One cannot understand race in the twentieth century unless one understands the life of Du Bois.

Lipschutz, Mark R. and R. Kent Rasmussen (1986). *Dictionary of African Historical Biography*. Berkeley: University of California Press.

An essential reference book for understanding "who's who" in Africa. Covers political, literary, and historical figures on the African continent.

Madhubuti, Haki (1980). *Black Men: Obsolete, Single, Dangerous?* Chicago: Third World Press.

The chapter on the books that all Africans need to read is worth the purchase itself. Madhubuti addresses a range of issues involving African men. A must for every library.

Mbiti, John S. (1975). *Introduction to African Religion*. London: Heinemann Press.

A fundamental book for understanding African religions. Mbiti also examines the influence of Christianity, Islam, and other religions on Africa, and how African religions have influenced so-called Western religions.

McGuire, Danielle (2010). *At the Dark End of the Street: Black Women, Rape, and Resistance—a New History of the Civil Rights Movement from Rosa Parks to the Rise of Black Power*. New York: Alfred A. Knopf.

This book finally explores what was difficult to write about a generation ago: that the rise of the civil rights movement was in part a response to the centuries-old sexual assault of African women. The horrors of unpunished sexual crimes against black women, executed against them by white men *and* white women, makes for gut-wrenching reading and reflection. It is essential reading for those who want to expand their knowledge of the "civil rights era."

Morrison, Toni (1987). *Beloved.* New York: Alfred A. Knopf.

The greatest African American love story ever told. Those who read it and don't understand it miss the emotional impact of slavery on Africans in America. Read it and read it again.

Morrison, Toni (1992). *Playing in the Dark: Whiteness and the Literary Imagination.* Cambridge, MA: Harvard University Press.

The importance of this book in understanding how Hawthorne, Melville, Twain, and other literary figures used Africans in developing American literature cannot be overestimated. Morrison's analysis of a new literary criticism based on understanding the "Africanization" of American literature is flawless and extraordinary.

Pieterse, Jan Nederveen (1992). *White on Black: Images of Africa and Blacks in Western Popular Culture.* New Haven, CT: Yale University Press.

A rare book that documents through extensive photographs and graphics how white supremacy was (is) interwoven throughout the history of European domination of the earth. The Dutch author's indictment of the cultural supports of white supremacy is rare among European social scientists.

Rediker, Marcus (2007). *The Slave Ship: A Human History.* New York: Viking.

Disagreements may exist about how many Africans were stolen and enslaved from Africa, but little disagreement emerges about the horrific and terrible machines—the slave ships—that transported them from the continent to the so-called "Western world." Rediker's gruesome and detailed history of the most barbaric machine ever invented to imprison humans must be read in doses. Few have devoted as much attention to what occurred during the infamous Middle Passage than Rediker. This book is a must-read for understanding the gory and loathsome efficiency of transporting more than sixty million human beings from their homeland to a life of enslavement in unknown lands.

Rowan, Carl (1996). *The Coming Race War in America.* New York: Little, Brown and Company.

A surprising and provocative book written by one of the world's leading black journalists. Rowan's final book outlines a chilling scenario of race relations in the world that pulls together a series of facts that alone make the book worthwhile reading.

Saxton, Alexander (1990). *The Rise and Fall of the White Republic.* London: Verso Press.

Saxton offers the hypothesis that the Americanization of nineteenth-century America was in actuality the conscious and deliberate attempt to structure a "white republic" that viewed all persons of color—Asians, Africans, and American Indians—as inferior.

Somé, Sobonfu (1999). *The Spirit of Intimacy: Ancient African Teachings in the Ways of Relationships.* New York: Quill/William Morrow.

Somé's small book is the only "marriage manual" that African people need. It challenges dearly held Western notions about marriage and relationships. Very profound and very readable.

Stamper, Norm (2005). *Breaking Rank: A Top Cop's Exposé of the Dark Side of American Policing.* New York: Nation Books.

The white former chief of police of San Diego tells why "police brutality" toward black people is not only routine but encouraged by a culture of fear of African men embedded in police departments not only in the United States, but around the world. A rare and honest disclosure of how racism is the motive behind most policing.

Umoja, Akinyele (2013). *We Will Shoot Back: Armed Resistance in the Mississippi Freedom Movement.* New York: NYU Press.

Robert Williams's classic book, *Negroes with Guns,* is now joined by Umoja's powerful history of the use of guns by American Africans during the civil rights era. The history of black armed self-defense has all but been ignored by those who wish to emphasize the "nonviolent" (passive?) nature of those who participated in the civil rights movement. This book explodes the myth that the use of guns was nonessential and virtually nonexistent in the liberation of African people in the United States.

Van Sertima, Ivan (1987, 1988). *African Presence in Early Europe* and *African Presence in Early Asia.* New Brunswick, NJ: Transaction Publishers.

Van Sertima traces early explorations into Europe and Asia by Africans. These works leave the reader with a broader understanding of how Africa has influenced the rest of the world.

Welsing, Frances Cress (1991). *The Isis Papers.* Chicago: Third World Press.

The number-one-selling nonfiction book among African Americans from 1991 to 1993. Welsing's thesis on the global system of white supremacy is still unchallenged. A most important book to read.

Williams, Chancellor (1976). *The Destruction of Black Civilization.* Chicago: Third World Press.

One of the most important books on why black civilizations declined from their former glory. Unsparing in his critique of those who raped the African continent, Williams seeks to understand the present through a deeper understanding of the past.

Wilson, Amos (1998). *Blueprint for Black Power.* New York: Afrikan World InfoSystems.

The indispensable handbook of black nationalism that should be read together with Marimba Ani's *Yurugu.* Wilson's book is the most comprehensive treatment of *how* to obtain "Black Power," the obstacles to obtaining it, and why it is the only logical and viable path to Afrikan liberation.

Winbush, Raymond (2009). *Belinda's Petition: A Concise History of Reparations for the TransAtlantic Slave Trade*. Philadelphia: XLibris Publishers.

The remarkable story of Belinda Royale, an enslaved African woman in Massachusetts in the late eighteenth century, illustrates the importance of understanding reparations as a constant theme in black redress during the past five hundred years. She won her case, and the book is a concise introduction to the reparations struggle waged by Africans throughout the world for justice perpetrated against them.

Winbush, Raymond (2003). *Should America Pay? Slavery and the Raging Debate on Reparations*. New York: Amistad/HarperCollins.

The struggle for reparations for enslaved Africans is as old as enslavement itself, having a distinct historical thread throughout the African world. This book brings together both supporters and opponents of reparations, and makes the strong case for why no "racial healing" will take place without justice being paid for the crime against humanity of African slavery.

Winbush, Raymond (2018). *The Warrior Method: A Parents' Guide to Rearing Healthy Black Boys*. New York: Amistad/HarperCollins.

Although discussing developmental issues confronting African boys, this book has wider implications for the need of all African people to understand their role in the *Maafa* and how white supremacy mediates the lives of African people all over the world. An indispensable book for understanding how to rear black children.

Woodson, Carter G. (1990). *The Miseducation of the Negro*. North Charleston, SC: CreateSpace Independent Publishing Platform.

The classic book offered by the "father" of African American history, on why blacks and whites have been miseducated.

Index

Raymond A. Winbush is research professor and director of the Institute for Urban Research at Morgan State University. He is the recipient of numerous grants, including a $2.6 million grant from the Kellogg Foundation to establish a "National Dialogue on Race" at Fisk University. He was a consultant and writer for the *Encyclopaedia Africana* project, is the former treasurer of the executive board of the National Council for Black Studies, and sits on the editorial board of the *Journal of Black Studies*.

ALSO BY
RAYMOND A. WINBUSH, PH.D

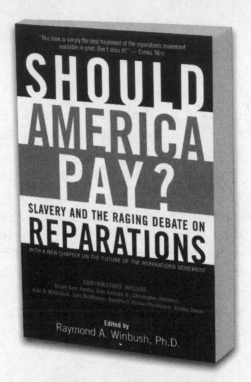

SHOULD AMERICA PAY?
Slavery and the Raging Debate on Reparations
Available in Paperback and eBook

"This book is simply the best treatment of the reparations movement available in print. Don't miss it!" —Cornel West

This comprehensive collection gathers together the seminal essays and key participants in the debate on reparations. Pro-reparations essays, including contributions by Congressman John Conyers Jr., Christopher Hitchens, and Professor Molefi Asante, are countered with arguments by Shelby Steele, Armstrong Williams, and John McWhorter, among others. Also featured are important documents, such as the First Congressional Reparations Bill of 1867 and the Dakar Declaration of 2001, as well as a new chapter on the current status and future direction of the movement.